SPIRITUAL HEALING

*as a Complement to the
Art of Medicine*

Madeleine and Tom Johanson

SPIRITUAL HEALING

as a Complement to the Art of Medicine

by

Madeleine Riedel-Michel

Translated from the German by Kay Gillioz-Pettigrew MIL

Regency Press (London & New York) Ltd.
125 High Holborn, London WC1V 6QA

This book is dedicated to my patients from all over the world and is intended to bring great light, joy and peace to the hearts of mankind. It is also hoped that it will encourage constructive co-operation between doctors, therapists, healers and patients.

Madeleine Riedel

ISBN 0 7212 0753 7

Printed and bound in Great Britain by
Buckland Press Ltd., Dover, Kent.

Contents

I. Autobiographical Notes

II. Fundamentals

Spiritual and Intellectual Powers (with exercises)

**The Seven Energy Centres (Chakras)
or the twelve portals (channels) corresponding in the subtle
body to the nervous and glandular systems in the physical**

**Where are these twelve Energy Centres (Channels) Located
and what is their Function?**

Spiritual Causes and Sources of our Sicknesses

A. In General

B. In Particular

Various Diseases and Conditions with Exercises to Activate the Appropriate Energy Centres

III. Reports and Contributions

IV. Letters of Acknowledgement

V. Interviews

VI. Spiritual Healing as a Complement to the Art of Medicine

Acknowledgements

So many people have contributed to this book in so many ways that it could quite simply never have been written without their help.

My most heartfelt thanks go to all of them—for their time and effort, for their friendship and encouragement and for their steadfast belief in a cause dear to all our hearts.

God bless you all,

Madeleine

Switzerland, October 1987

Note

A C60 tape is available direct from the publishers at £5.95 post free
  Side one: Healing Meditation and Activation of the 12 Energy
            Centres
  Side two: Release from Worry and Anxiety through Relaxation

Foreword

This is a very unusual book, being out of the ordinary in both form and content. The author is not an experienced writer but is and always will be, as she herself says, "A simple, ordinary woman". Consequently, the intellectually oriented reader will find this book lacking in all rhyme and reason, with neither logical structure nor systematic sub-division—the expression of a "naive faith" and a "childlike light-heartedness".

But if people are prepared without question to accept faith and childlikeness in, say, a nun, they might be expected to tolerate them in a healer, particularly when precisely these characteristics appear to be an essential element of her exceptional healing ability.

Those, therefore, who from the start are prepared to forego any attempt to understand this book with their heads but, rather, to allow their hearts to be moved by the abundance of experience it communicates, and those willing to rejoice at the kaleidoscopic diversity of all this book describes will reap great reward from their reading.

Anyone personally acquainted with Madeleine Riedel knows that any pompous seeking for recognition, not to mention unreliable boastfulness, would be entirely alien to her nature; she reports too little rather than too much. And if the reader finds some things over-exuberant or exaggerated, he should bear in mind that he would doubtless create a similar impression if he were called upon to describe, say, the indescribable impression of an exceptional natural phenomenon or a glorious work of art to someone who had never seen or experienced anything of the kind.

We must, therefore, carefully bear in mind that the contents of this book are solely factual accounts of things we can no longer disregard with a shrug of the shoulders, no matter how incredible they may seem. In view of facts such as these the only appropriate approach, precisely on the part of a conscientious scientist seeking earnestly after truth, is their unprejudiced examination.

Let us, therefore, take the hand Mrs. Riedel proffers and comply with her request to accord her constructive co-operation and a fair appreciation of her activity instead of persisting in negative criticism and destructive rejection. It is high time that acquired medical knowledge and endowed natural ability, intellect and intuition, rationality and spirituality join hands for the benefit of suffering humanity.

Dr. Hans Endres

Introduction

Heaven be thanked for the gift of healing.

This book is intended to show the reader how to take the first step towards health and the healing of sickness. I am writing this book because of the need I feel to help all those who are prepared to be helped. However, a healthy body presupposes a healthy spirit and here there is urgent need for reorientation. This book can also help those who believe there is no hope for them.

Consequently, you should read this book slowly, pausing after each chapter. You should think over what you have read and, above all, digest it all carefully. It may often be necessary to re-read certain passages to make sure the sense be clearly understood.

The thoughts I set down here are nothing sensational and I am straining for no effect. I describe the signs I have witnessed and which have served to point my way. May they also serve all those of goodwill to understand the knowledge thus vouchsafed of healing which Divine Power renders possible.

At the same time, however, new opportunities should also be opened up. I feel it should be possible to place these wonderful healing forces and classical medicine and surgery side by side. My aim is, therefore, also to put forward the idea of co-operation to open-minded doctors, surgeons and medical students. Examples of co-operation of this kind where doctors work with me towards the recovery of patients would then prove that reorientation on the part of all concerned be both possible and effective.

For twenty-three years I have been a spiritual healer by vocation. It is a source of great joy when I can serve fellow human beings seeking help. Throughout all these years thousands of despairing, lost people, sick in body, mind and soul, have sought relief and help in my practice for spiritual healing in Lenzburg. At first I simply made my healing powers available to all who sought me out. Knowing myself to be an

instrument of God, I invested all my strength. Today, however, I
believe that, with a little more understanding, a great deal more could
be achieved. In other words, the success of healing would be even
greater if co-operation between patient, doctor and healer could be
realized.

I come from a family of healers and I have had healing in my blood,
so to speak, since childhood. My father, the famous healer and
hypnotist, Hermano, did pioneer work in curing people of smoking
during the 1970s. In the next chapter I shall describe in detail the single
event which made me become a healer. My basic training in healing
lasted ten years and was given me by my father. At his side I healed
independently and rejoiced at my successes. My training was more than
the mere communication of knowledge; it was the transmission of
practices that had in a way been handed down to initiates from
generation to generation. I tried to advance on this basis. I intensified
my studies and took great interest in visiting spiritual healing centres in
South America and on the Philippines.

I also tried to further my knowledge of medicine. The culminating
point of my life was my meeting on the Philippines with the psychic
surgeon, Josephine Sison. But I shall be talking about this in a later
chapter.

The circumstance that I am reporting on my life's aim and the
possibilities provided by spiritual healing, and that I wish to
communicate to a wider circle of interested readers all that I can hardly
wait to say, is due to a second meeting with the well-known English
healer, Tom Johanson. We met for the first time in Josephine Sison's
big chapel on the Philippines and again during a conference on
"Doctors and Healers" in Zurich.

It must first be said that Tom Johanson, with his straightforward
manner and, above all, his positive radiation, woke in me the idea of
setting down my experiences and ideas and making them accessible to
those interested.

It seems to me that the time has come when patient, doctor and
healer could follow a common path towards restoring suffering patients
to health. One thing is certain—healers and doctors would have to form
a close-knit team enjoying total mutual confidence if this idea is ever to
become reality. There is already proof that, in this direction, much
would change for the better. In 1982 the first international healers'
symposium, NATURA, was held in Basle, in conjunction with an

exhibition on healthy living. Well-known healers from England, the Philippines and Switzerland collaborated in this event and it was a signal success. In 1982 Swiss television showed a film on the subject of "Healing Hands". More than ten thousand enquiries were received from viewers.

The particularly important factor in this evolution seems to me that this special art of healing be brought to the attention of the public and that doctors be invited to participate; another important thing is that successes be conscientiously monitored in order to eliminate charlatans right from the start.

A further incentive to launch out on my literary work and realize my idea of describing the essential nature of spiritual healing was certainly my healing meditation sessions (in groups of 12-30 persons and in halls holding 40-400 persons).

Between Spring 1983 and Spring 1984 I held sessions of this kind on Saturdays and Sundays for patients and seekers after help. It is worthy of note here that, for the first time, doctors, psychologists, nurses, philosophers, medical students, scientists and clergymen were among these groups. In this context I should like to express my most heartfelt gratitude to all those who have made articles available to me. May their work bring help to many and contribute towards promoting mutual understanding to the common good.

Madeleine Riedel

I. Autobiographical Notes

My childhood at the side of a famous father and a self-effacing, devoted mother, amidst my ten brothers and sisters

My childhood was interesting, tempestuous and altogether exceptional and these early years put their imprint on my whole life.

When I was young I had to get used to the idea that my father "could do more than other people". Indeed, my brothers and sisters and I had to learn very early that people who practised healing or hypnosis were loved and respected by many but also despised and ousted by doubters and wrong-thinkers.

As a child I already felt sorry for these doubters. How little they knew of my father! He was a deeply believing man blessed by a gift from God for which he was grateful. I would often see him kneeling on his faldstool in silent prayer, immersed in deep gratitude. At that time, as Hermano, he gave many performances as a hypnotist throughout Switzerland. Particularly at the Corso in Zurich he filled the halls for weeks and even months, fascinating the public with his unusual experiments in hypnosis. He always allowed us children to take part in all these activities and we therefore grew up in a mystical world which we accepted without question.

Later on my father devoted himself exclusively to the suffering and those seeking help. He let his healing power flow through them and they were cured. People came to him from all over the world seeking advice and assistance in unusual situations or healing for their ills.

In the Gospel according to *St. Mark*, chapter 16, verse 18, it is written, ". . . they shall lay hands on the sick and they shall recover."

For many years he also undertook experiments in telepathy, in co-operation with the police, and many people who were missing after the War were found and sometimes whole families were reunited as a result. I lost count of how many times we were forced to move house and change schools just because my father practised healing. In those days people must have read the Bible with their eyes closed to have seen so little that was Christian in my father's work.

How and why I became a healer; my paralysis in South America

Once more we had been forced to face up to yet another move and even a change of language since we landed for a time in South America, in Santiago de Chile.

For me, at the tender age of nine and for my seven brothers and sisters this new country was mysterious and fascinating but also fraught with danger. But together we were strong and we discovered whatever there was to be discovered along forbidden paths.

I used to slip under the tall garden fence and felt thoroughly at home among the natives, the (half-breed) Chileans and the Indians. They poured upon me endless love and kindness and since that time I have retained a deep affection for the Indians.

One day an epidemic of smallpox and typhus broke out. At school the children had to stand in line to be vaccinated at high speed. The following day four of the children at our school were completely paralyzed; one of them was me.

There I lay, desperate, my little body paralyzed. The days passed and became weeks and then months.

It was during this time that I began to enter into a deeper relationship with our Creator. I began talking to Him and His angels and these conversations finally became an accepted thing. A deep inner strength awoke in my soul and slowly grew in intensity. Through the spiritual exercises my father taught me my consciousness was heightened. I started to leave my body and my soul went journeying; I also began to recognize the human aura more frequently and in a greater variety of colours. I developed clairvoyant abilities although, as a child, I felt these were more a trial than a blessing.

However, I recall that I had but a single burning desire—to run, to climb, to turn somersaults and cartwheels and once more to play and chase about with my brothers and sisters.

One day, as I communed deeply with God, I had a vision which told me that I should become a healer and must follow this path until I died; that, whatever befell me, I should always have God's protection and that I should slowly recover in body and spirit. I was deeply moved and filled with gratitude. I told no one of what had occurred except, later on, my father who had contributed so much to my recovery. My mother's loving care and attention, her unfaltering belief in my recovery and the strength of her positive thinking also played an important role.

And I recovered. Later on we returned to Switzerland and lived in Heiden in Canton Appenzell for seven years. My father had a large practice there and he also ran a thirty-bed "Kurhaus", a hotel where people came for treatment. We youngsters did our best to help.

One day a Dr. Siegrist, at that time a member of the cantonal government, came to my father with a slipped disc. He knew all about my father's homesickness for his native canton of Aargau. Dr. Siegrist promised my father that, if he cured him, he would enable him to practise once again in Aargau. Dr. Siegrist recovered and kept his word.

Peace and quiet in Lenzburg

In 1958 my father sold all he possessed in Canton Appenzell and, thanks to Dr. Siegrist's recovery, moved to Lenzburg, taking his eleven children with him.

I should like to take this opportunity of expressing my deep gratitude to the people of Lenzburg and to their mayor, Arnold Hirt, who has since died, to his successor, Dr. Hans Theiler, and to the present mayor or "Stadtamman", Albin Härdi, for the circumstance that we found a home here in Lenzburg and were allowed to pursue our healing activities without any difficulties being raised by the local authorities, the police or the local people. Every single day that I spend here is for me a priceless gift.

Working with my father

My father and I had long talks during my childhood and once, when we broached the subject of love, I told him a little anxiously that he had given me too big a heart, that I passed on this gift of love to everyone I met as he had always taught me but that there was still a lot of room left in my heart. My father gazed thoughtfully into the middle distance during this recital; then his deep blue eyes focussed and, taking my hand in his, he said, "Look, the time will come when you will be able to give all this tremendous love to innumerable sick people."

How right he was! At barely twenty-one I became a totally committed healer by vocation. He took me into his practice and I worked there seven hours a day to help and to heal the sick, despondent and desperate people who came to our practice in Lenzburg from all over the world. At my father's side I healed independently, knowing full well that I was only an instrument of God. My father was a good teacher and he initiated me into the secrets that are handed down from generation to generation.

On 19th July, 1963, when my father was abroad, he wrote me an important letter that could be of significance for many healers and doctors. "You are, perhaps, sometimes amazed at your successes. These are due to the circumstance that you are committed heart and soul to your work. The sick do not seek learned talk and seeming knowledge but merely human affection and moral support. Go on using this method and not only will your patients respect you but—far more important—you will find complete satisfaction in your work."

Madeleine's Parents

There is no better thing on earth than to be at peace with oneself, with God and the world. Our work is also an excellent way of learning how best to cope with everyday living. We learn to do certain things at certain times, to control ourselves and to repress certain personal moods; above all, we learn to serve people, with all their virtues and weaknesses, in their hope for help, in their search for support in this increasingly lonely world. By being something to others we become something to ourselves. The more of yourself you invest in others, the greater your own strength will become. Our Creator speaks to us through His Son, "Inasmuch as ye have done it unto one of the least of these my brethren, ye have done it unto me" (The Gospel according to *St. Matthew*, chapter 25, verse 40).

Separation from my father

For ten years we worked together. He taught me a great deal and initiated me. But one day he intimated that he would like to continue alone and that he saw a new and important task ahead. From then on he devoted himself entirely to curing people of smoking.

Dr. Mario Gmür of the Medical Research Institute in Zurich accompanied him for a long time wherever he went to treat people. A record was kept of everything and the patients were asked to fill out questionnaires and to return them after a certain time. This prompted Dr. Gmür to write his dissertation, *How Hermano Breaks the Smoking Habit by the Laying On of Hands*.

This triggered a tremendous wave of breaking the smoking habit. Curers of the smoking habit shot out of the ground like mushrooms. It had needed a pioneer like Hermano to give others courage.

My father was asked to go to many countries where he released the staffs of whole factories and hospitals from their nicotine qualm. Doctors became interested in these cures and Hermano received many tokens of recognition from all sides since his method proved the most successful.

My father's death

Like everyone else a healer must die in due time. This is difficult for many people to understand—they seem to think things should go on unchanged for a hundred years or so. But God gathers us all in sooner or later, a circumstance we must humbly accept. My father died at the age of sixty-two on the 7th January, 1979, after having told my mother he wanted to sleep his fill. He died quietly in his sleep, well prepared for Eternity.

At this time I was in Jamaica, in the Caribbean, with my children. My daughter, Isabella, went home earlier than the rest of us since she had to return to school.

Here I should like once more to draw the reader's attention to thought transference. Many of you will have received a sign at the time a loved one has died—be it that a voice was heard or an apparition seen, that the clock stopped or a flowerpot broke, a picture fell from the wall at this particular moment or a dog began to howl; these are just some of the possible phenomena.

I, too, was able precisely to note the hour of my father's death; but not only I—several of my brothers and sisters even suffered severe abdominal pain. I told my son that Papa was dead, that I felt it and that we should make our flight reservations in order to get home as soon as possible. So that, when my sister, Thesy, telephoned, she did no more than confirm precisely what I already knew.

We flew home. On my arrival I was overcome by a terrible inability to think or act. I sought out a good friend, Dr. Alfred Bühler, and shall never forget how grieved he was by my father's death. With a few well-chosen words he helped me on my way and sent me to my mother. She was expecting me. Her grief was boundless—after all, she had led a richly rewarding life at my father's side for more than forty years.

My attitude towards death has always been positive and wholesome and this helped me through the weeks that followed.

My own activity

Every healer has an individual way of working depending on how his personality develops. People often ask me how I have managed to expend so much energy day in, day out for twenty-three years. My reply is always the same—"It is not I who heal but God. I am merely His instrument. Thank Him, not me."

I should like to explain here, as best I can, just how I work.

It is tremendously important to me that the patient not only be cured of the symptoms of his illness but also that he learn to consider his way of life, to recognize the origin of his malady and to apply his new-found awareness to bringing about a positive change in his way of thinking. He must learn to have confidence in himself and his state of health. He must recognize that in sickness lie suffering, darkness and fear and in health, light, joy, love, strength and self-realization. That is to say that he must contribute towards rediscovering his joy in living, taking pleasure in such simple things as flowers, grasses, woods, the sky and people, in singing and laughing with them. He must try to understand everything and to adopt a positive attitude to it all.

My activity always commences with a little ceremony I consider important. My day begins very early with meditation and prayer wherein I always include all those I know and love and the cares and problems of my patients, sending thoughts of light, love, strength and peace out into the world.

Before starting work I always say the prayer of St. Francis of Assisi (see page 47) as it is instinct with the humility which must imbue every healer at work, no matter how successful he be. I then recite a psalm from the Bible in German, English or a Filipino dialect, as the spirit moves me. Then I touch the flag given me by the psychic surgeon, Josephine Sison, when I was accepted as a member of and initiated into the Filipino association of healers on 31st January, 1981. I lay my hands over the Swiss and Filipino soil I have collected and keep in jars. Then I prayerfully await inspiration, raising my hands, palms upwards, to Heaven. For a while I let the Divine power flow through me. I sing all the while and put myself entirely into God's hands.

This little ceremony serves to put my private life entirely to one side. It elevates me to a higher level of spiritual awareness which enables me, as one with God, to serve my sick brethren as His instrument from eight to ten hours each day. The ceremony also creates a positive field of vibrations in the room where I work and the energy this affords makes me capable of peak performance.

After about three hours I consolidate this state through brief spiritual exercises and prayer.

Then the patients arrive, one after the other, and I listen to their cares and problems. There is often no need for words since I am able to recognize disruptive influences via the patient's aura and can treat him accordingly. This creates a relationship of great confidence. With the patient sitting or lying down I let healing power flow through him, always to the accompaniment of silent prayer and relaxing music.

I speak telepathically to the cells and organs as if they were my friends, for cells and organs have a means of understanding. I instruct them to let healthy cells take over from the sick ones and I tell them that this will lead to the recovery of good health. It is clear that the longer the patient has been ill, the more treatments will be necessary since every healing process is basically a process of learning.

How often in the course of my spiritual healing activity have I seen that the true causes of disease are lust for power, tyranny, inconsideration, indifference, meanness in everyday life and lack of mutual understanding in the family and at work. All embittered, depressive, downtrodden, frustrated, resigned, spiritually battered people really fall sick because of a lack of love. They were never allowed to experience the true, tender, tranquil and sensitive love that is so beautifully described in the *First Letter to the Corinthians*, chapter 13, verses 4-8:

"Charity suffereth long and is kind; charity envieth not; charity vaunteth not itself, is not puffed up.

Doth not behave itself unseemly, seeketh not her own, is not easily provoked, thinketh no evil;

Rejoiceth not in iniquity, but rejoiceth in the truth;

Beareth all things, believeth all things, endureth all things.

Charity never faileth: but whether there be prophecies, they shall fail; whether there be tongues, they shall cease; whether there be knowledge, it shall vanish away."

How often have politicians and business managers brought me their seriously stricken wives for treatment, demanding a "miracle as quickly as possible"! All these husbands tell me that their wives have everything they could possibly desire—plenty of money, a car, elegant clothes, a house, children, a busy social life—their every conceivable wish is fulfilled and still they become sicker and sicker and more and more dissatisfied. If one talks to these women one finds that while, on the one hand, they outwardly possess an over-abundance of material things, on the other they are suffering from serious spiritual privation. They "couldn't care less" about all the money, about the politics and the national economy that have left such an arctic climate in their wake and wrought havoc with these women's private lives. They want one thing only—that their husbands spend more time with them and pay them more attention; that they be enabled to nurture a true partnership. But because their husbands are not prepared to fulfil precisely these desires since their heads are full of other, for them far more pressing matters, their wives unconsciously enslave them by falling ill. And the more serious the illness the better these wives are able to keep their husbands at their sides. They triumph because their husbands have at last been forced to find time to preoccupy themselves on their wives' account.

This is, however, an unhealthy and dangerous game since it leads to self-destruction and also to destruction of the partner. It requires enormous tact, sensitivity and understanding to help people in this situation since one must point out to both partners the error of their ways and unlock their hardened hearts. I explain to them that they are not entitled to demand more of the other than they themselves are able to give. They should slowly but surely disinter the love they have buried and discover each other anew. But Nature always has a compensatory effect: the present economic crisis and unemployment will automatically help these people since, suddenly, money is no longer flowing so abundantly through their hands. They are forced once more to take notice of each other; they now have time for each other.

Even if we do not much like the idea, we know perfectly well that the big crises in the world are the results of our own actions, for God gave us freedom of will and we have abused it. It is not God who has forsaken us, but we who have turned away from him!

Let us in future be spiritually more aware and daily expand our consciousness. Let us look to the future and raise our hearts once again to God. Let us confess Him from the bottom of our hearts, each according to his beliefs. Let us together send out thoughts of light, love, power and peace to the hearts of all humankind, to the domain of politics and the economy, in order that the terrible world-political iciness be thawed and sensible, beneficial decisions be taken.

How one becomes a healer

The following are the characteristics of every spiritual healer:

Compassionate understanding and consistent investment of one's life in humanity as a whole. Spiritual, psychic gifts. An overriding vocation; one is called by God. A profound humility that may never be set aside no matter how successful the healer may be. A deep love for suffering humanity since love is the source of all healing.

You must have a strong personality, an upright character, patience and nerves of steel. The greater your faith in God, the better you will be able to stand up to the inevitable storms and outside attacks. You must constantly be aware that you are an instrument of God, His "channel". You regard healing as your life's work and are prepared to make great sacrifices and forego a great deal in your private life.

You may on no account gain profit from these activities. You must refrain from advertisement since this would only arouse envy, jealousy and greed in others. A healer by vocation will never need to advertise since his patients will be sent by God and those whom a healer helps will broadcast this good work and send other sufferers to him.

It is advisable and courageous to work on a donation basis so as to enable those in financial straits to obtain regular treatment. I am thinking here of the unemployed, the desperate and the faint-hearted who need spiritual and physical renewal to enable them once again to face the future. Furthermore, adoption of an attitude and system such as this is appropriate to the humility required of a healer. I have also had occasion to discover that doctors work far more readily with spiritual healers who apply this system of donation.

Regular meditation and a sensible mode of life, no smoking, very moderate consumption of alcohol and vegetarian nutrition should become second nature since all these factors increase your vital energy and healing powers and help you to remain in harmony with yourself and with God. Your body is entitled to long forest walks and a certain amount of sport since the demands made upon it by your healing activities require this much compensation.

Do not despair if you are not accepted in the place where you live or even by your close family and more distant relatives. You will have to learn that everyone is entitled to his own opinion. Always remember Jesus Christ:

"And when He was come into His own country, He taught them in their synagogue, insomuch that they were astonished, and said, whence hath this man this wisdom, and these mighty works?

And they were offended in Him. But Jesus said unto them, A prophet is not without honour, save in his own country, and in his own house.

And He did not many mighty works there because of their unbelief." (The Gospel according to St. Matthew, chapter 13, verses 54, 57-58).

Should there be brief moments of despair and despondency, these words should help you. They have carried me forward throughout my life and have strengthened me in my contemplation of the future.

The knowledge that nothing can be achieved by insistence also seems to me to be important; you must allow yourself many years for your spiritual development. Let these psychic gifts grow in you since it is only your endless patience, love and goodness and your profound trust in God that will bring you the resolution and the endurance necessary to accomplish such a tremendous task as that to which you are devoting your life.

*   *   *

My life and spiritual work in the Philippines

Before I flew to the Philippines for my first stay in 1980/81 I went very deeply into the question of psychic surgery, as it was called at the time. Today one speaks of logurgy. I already knew a little about this phenomenon from the Indians and I wanted to learn more.

I studied the parapsychological film, *In*, and saw all the other films that had been made on the subject. I went to the lectures and read the books by Dr. Stelter, Dr. Hans Nägeli and Rudolf Passian.

Rudolf Passian also gave me the addresses of the best-known healers and this helped me to become acquainted with them much more quickly.

This tropical island realm with its 7,107 islands and approximately forty-seven million inhabitants fascinated me right from the start; I even felt as if I had "come home" to this mystical, spiritual world I love so well.

It was during my fourth sojourn in this "Land of Smiles", which is also affectionately called "The Pearl of the Orient", that I wrote this book. This time the psychic surgeon, Josephine Sison, had invited me to stay for three and a half months. Here I devoted myself to the poorest of the poor, to the sick and the desperate out in the countryside and up in the mountains. I adapted myself entirely to the local people, living, eating and working with them.

They were always friendly, relaxed and gay, living and enjoying each moment as it came, and where guitar music was to be heard many Filipinos would gather and listen spellbound to the music. They never cross their bridges before they get to them, although they are very, very poor and would have sufficient reason to worry about tomorrow. But at a temperature of 40°C worrying would require far too much effort!

Here the people have not yet been ruined by materialism. If you constantly share their country and mountainlife with these people, you soon learn to understand why so many spiritual healers and an occasional psychic surgeon emerge in these islands.

Here, in the Province of Ouirino, in the mountains and caves where, this time, I spent five weeks with Josephine Sison and her team, I had exactly the same experience I had had as a child among the Indians in South America.

I learnt to converse with the snakes, beetles and spiders and also with the "Encantos", the natural spirits to be found in the mountains, caves, forests, rocks and waters.

The local people also believe in the "Anitos", the spirits they evoke in their religious ceremonies.

Their close contact with Nature awakens an intuitive awareness in these people which makes them particularly lovable. This doubtless explains why one feels so secure among them so quickly.

When one has seen for oneself mothers and their babies participating in hour-long sessions so that the children automatically grow up in a spiritual context and, as of the age of eight, can already become spiritual mediums, one is no longer surprised that these people, who are already mystic by nature, are able to reach an increased level of paranormal awareness much more quickly than we Europeans.

The spiritual healers and psychic surgeons practise mainly in the Province of Pangasinan on the Island of Luzon, in the direction of Manila, Carmen, Villasis, Urdaneta and Baguio. Here there is particularly favourable earth radiation in conjunction with a great deal of water, salt and sunshine which are alleged to be of great importance in healing and particularly in operations.

It is also said that the Filipinos are descended from the Lemurians and that, at one time, the centre of the Lemurian civilization was situated in the Province of Pangasinan, that is to say where psychic surgery is practised today and also where Josephine Sison and many other psychic surgeons of my acquaintance live and work.

I can confirm this from personal experience since, as a healer working in this region, I was daily aware of being in a field of intensified vibration and I felt the positive earth radiation, the water and the salt nearby and let the rays of the sun flow through me. Whether I was working alone or with Josephine, I was capable of peak performance in spite of the tropical heat.

(This is also why I worked on this book only in the Philippines, in the Pangasinan region and in the mountains, near the caves.)

There are many spiritual healers in the Philippines but only about thirty to thirty-five psychic surgeons. That is very few in a country with forty-seven million inhabitants and this proves that one cannot just quickly learn psychic surgery as many Europeans believe.

God alone knows why these signs and wonders can be wrought by only a very few people that He has chosen!

The First Epistle to the Corinthians, chapter 12, verses 4-11, will help you better to understand this:

"Now there are diversities of gifts, but the same Spirit. And there are differences of administrations, but the same Lord.

And there are diversities of operations, but it is the same God which worketh all in all.

But the manifestations of Spirit is given to every man to profit withal.

For to one is given by the Spirit the word of wisdom; to another the word of knowledge by the same Spirit;

To another faith by the same Spirit; to another the gift of healing by the same Spirit;

To another the working of miracles; to another prophecy; to another discerning of spirits; to another divers kinds of tongues; to another the interpretation of tongues;

But all these worketh that one and the selfsame spirit, dividing to every man severally as he will."

There are a great many spiritually oriented associations in the Philippines. These are called "Union Espritista Cristiana de Filipinas". If one wishes to become a member of one of these associations one must devote oneself to profound study of the Bible and lead an irreproachable spiritual life.

Once psychic abilities have manifested themselves in the course of regular, weekly sessions, the person concerned is rapidly encouraged until yet another gift appears. If a "Medium Operador" (psychic surgeon) is discovered—an occurrence that is extremely rare—the members of his family and all those around him are more careful than ever to ensure that this new medium lead a spiritually oriented life and be exposed as little as possible to all the earthly temptations of daily life in order that, in future, he may devote himself entirely to this responsible work. People of this kind are particularly respected, supported during the sessions by means of beautiful, spiritual singing and helped in every possible way to become an instrument in the Divine "channel".

He is relieved of a large number of everyday tasks he performed before because "he now has more important things to do". Word quickly gets about when a new "Medium Operador" is born. People tell each other the news with respect and awe.

Furthermore, the local people depend upon these spiritual healers and psychic surgeons since they are much too poor to contribute to sickness benefit societies.

Just as a battery occasionally needs recharging, every healer goes to the caves in the mountains where he remains for long periods of time deeply immersed in prayer and meditation in order to renew his healing powers.

There are various types of medium in the Philippines:
1. Psychic surgeons. 2. Healing mediums. 3. Spiritual healers who practise teletherapy. 4. Clairvoyant mediums. 5. Writing mediums. 6. Prophetic mediums. 7. Palm-reading mediums. 8. Aura-seeing mediums. 9. Mediums who see past incarnations.

Healing and operation

In divine healing the patient and the healer sit and pray together for healing.

In magnetic healing the healer transmits his energy to the patient.

In psychic or spiritual (telepathic) healing the emission of the healer's spiritual power of positive thought to the soul of the sufferer brings about a positive physical change.

In psychic surgery the "Medium Operador" intervenes manually directly in the body, whereby the medium's own exceptional energy penetrates a kind of magnetic field which holds the cell structure of the human body together. He usually commences with his index or middle finger and the energy is aimed at loosening the cell structure of the affected part of the body, at changing or even temporarily "dissolving" it so that the medium can penetrate the body wall without difficulty.

I have often seen that a great deal of blood gushes and there is a correspondingly unpleasant odour, particularly in patients who are heavy smokers. Subsequently blood formations, cysts, small tumours, etc. are eliminated. When the medium's finger is withdrawn from the body the magnetic field automatically closes behind it again so that there is no wound. It is a question here of materialization where the "Medium Operador" treats the "invisible counterpart" of the body. We call this the astral body. If the astral body is healed the healing can take effect in the physical body.

With regard to sterile conditions, it has been scientifically proved on numerous occasions that the magnetic fields surrounding the hands of the healer ("Medium Operador") are so strong that they virtually disinfect the area around the "wound". Anyone interested in knowing more about the scientific aspects of psychic surgery in the Philippines should read the book, *Psychic Surgery in the Philippines* by the Swiss doctor, Hans Nägerli-Osjord (Leuchter Verlag, Otto Reichl, Ramagen).

My sojourn in the mountain caves on the Philippines

When, at the beginning of 1982, the psychic surgeon, Josephine Sison, insisted absolutely that I share her pre-Pascal cave retreat, I knew intuitively that this was to be the most important event in my life. Indeed, I felt that it would forge my future and afford me indescribable, unforgettable and profound spiritual experiences.

It is a tradition with Josephine Sison that, three or four weeks before Easter or during Holy Week, healers from at home and abroad, chosen and invited by her, meet in the caves to regenerate their healing powers that have been weakened by the influence of everyday life.

In Diseluad, in the tropical Philippine mountains, outside the town of Aglipay in the Province of Quirino, to the north-east of Manila, there are twelve caves, each more beautiful and full of adventure than the other.

The following are brief extracts from my diary for 1982 and 1984.

1982

There are about seventy-two of us (eight people from abroad and the rest local people). For fifteen days and nights we have been living in profound silence. We are permitted to speak only seven words each day. This is very hard for me since I have a thousand questions at the tip of my tongue! But Josephine told me to "Go where it is quiet and be silent for there you will find all the answers". How right she was! By the end of the retreat I had indeed found all the answers in meditation. I fast all the time, thus cleansing body, soul and spirit. Up here we lead a rucksack and sleeping-bag existence and are housed at "headquarters", outside Caves Nos. I, II and III. Water must be fetched from a great distance and only very little remains each day for our personal ablutions.

There is no electric light so we live in darkness with just our candles and torches. I have gone barefoot so long that I feel I have reverted to the primitive state. We all sleep on the floor in the same room, jockeying for space, especially when there is a thunderstorm—our huts have neither windowpanes nor shutters and the wind drives the rain straight into our faces! In the end we sleep standing up until the storm has passed. We lead a simple but profoundly spiritual life that I could wish might become a permanence. In the evenings, refreshed by the prayer, singing and deep meditation in the caves, we go to "head-quarters" where, by candlelight, we treat many of the native people who have come from distant villages to obtain advice, help or healing.

We are accompanied by a young woman doctor and her husband from Belgium, a man and a woman healer from Australia, a married couple, both healers, from the USA and a woman therapist from Geneva; all of them are greatly impressed.

1984

Because of the consecration by Josephine Sison on 18th April of the new chapel, "El Paraiso del Progresso", rather more local and foreign guests than usual had been invited, about 400 people altogether.

This time we had a certain amount of electric light and a water pump so that appreciably more water was available. Only a few had fasted this time. I fasted for five days because I felt the cleansing to be important. The others were too excited to fast. Silence was not imposed upon us this time. We had with us a small flock of specially chosen, psychically-gifted children aged upwards of eight years who were to be further trained by us throughout the whole five weeks. It is therefore not to be wondered at that children such as these later become good healers, perhaps even psychic surgeons, after having been launched, so to speak, by the deeply moving experience of these cave sojourns which they are even able to repeat each year. It is good to know that these children are destined to become tomorrow's spiritual healers. The consecration on Wednesday, 18th April, was a great event, as was also the symbolic washing of feet on Maundy Thursday that we were permitted to witness in Cave No. I and the Lord's Last Supper in Cave No. II on Good Friday. Doctors, acupuncturists, healers, priests, politicians and civil servants from France, the USA, Canada, Australia, Alaska, Japan and the Philippines and myself from Switzerland—people from the most varied professions and confessions—shared the experience of a great, spiritual step forward, forming a single harmonious unit and generating a powerful field of vibration by their positive thought. Together we sent out light, love and peace to the world. Let us take this opportunity of recalling that unity will be the clearly recognizable characteristic of humanity when people *themselves* one day tear down the separating walls and banish the barriers between one race and another, one people and another, one religion and another—indeed, between one human being and another.

Each day we visited another cave. A prayer for protection and another of gratitude are said before entering and leaving a cave. Inside the cave we remained for hours in silence, meditating, praying and fasting, cleansing our bodies, souls and spirits; we contemplated the sufferings of Jesus Christ and swung on the wings of our spiritual songs to a state where we crossed the space-time barrier.

Dear reader, go and sit in some quiet corner and imagine you are with me in the cave. Here, in the utter silence, intuitive comprehension comes alive. We listen compliantly for the voice of truth that shows the way and experience a powerful field of vibration that carries us into the broad light of knowledge and truth and grants us the revelations of the Holy Spirit. In profound peace and silence we feel the purity and light of divine fulfilment and abandon ourselves to the rhythms of the spiritual world, accompanied by the scents of the burning candles and the uplifting, devoted singing of the children; we experience a tremendous expansion of consciousness during the hours we spend beyond the space-time barrier. Our restricting ego releases us and we experience the endless horizons of our souls and the eternal love of Almighty God; we are immersed in the security of our affirmative being.

"Praise ye the Lord. Praise God in His sanctuary: praise Him in the firmament of His power.

Praise Him for His mighty acts: praise Him according to His excellent greatness.

Praise Him with the sound of the trumpet: praise Him with the psaltery and harp.

Praise Him with the timbrel and dance: praise Him with stringed instruments and organs.

Praise Him upon the loud cymbals: praise Him upon the high sounding cymbals.

Let everything that hath breath praise the Lord. Praise ye the Lord."
(*Psalm* 150)

South America

In Brazil spiritual healing and psychic surgery are enormously widespread. It is best to contact a medical-spiritual healing centre which gives addresses of healers in the heartland. In Brazil I met the parapsychologist and writer, Rudolf Passian, and his companion, the medium, Irene Schlenk. We planned to spend three weeks visiting these exceptional phenomena, an undertaking which proved successful thanks to good contact addresses and the protection of two stalwart policemen, for Brazil is a dangerous country. What is more, these mediums often work and may be visited only at night unless they are at a healing centre. We were greatly impressed by the medical-spiritual healing centre in Rio de Janeiro where, on several occasions, we were allowed by Dr. Massena, the psychiatrist in charge, to spend some time. Professionally and socially highly placed persons do auxiliary work at this centre as voluntary healers. We spent several hours there on each visit and were also permitted to help with the healing. The proceedings opened with a long introductory speech. Since Rudolf Passian is well-known and much loved at this healing centre, a long speech of welcome was addressed to him. The hall was always entirely filled by those seeking help. Then fifteen mediums at a time sat at a table and were given photographs of people seeking aid and reports of others suffering harsh destinies. Through prayer followed by classical music these mediums went into a trance and teletherapy began. Later on we met the famous (spiritual) medium, Luiz Gasparette, in Sao Paulo, a young man who works as a psychologist at a hospital. As soon as he goes into a trance he paints portraits and landscapes by dead artists—Potinari, Renoir, Degas, Delacroix, Toulouse-Lautrec, van Gogh, Modigliani, Aleijadinho, Anita Malfatti, Lasar Segal, Michelangelo, Raphael, Tarsilade Amaral, Picasso, Manet, Matisse, Tissit, Dumet, Goya, Gauguin, Boticelli and others—at great speed and without a paintbrush, using only his hands and fingers.

On our first visit he took us to his studio where he told us the story of his life and showed us a great many pictures from his collection. Every picture he paints is auctioned and the proceeds used for benevolent purposes. At that time he had already painted about 4000 pictures which are in great demand in parapsychological circles. He invited us to attend one of his manifestations. Accompanied by the chief police surgeon, our two policemen and some astrologist friends, we drove to a remote place where about 2000 people awaited Luiz Gasparette's demonstration. A lady journalist gave a long introductory explanation. Then the light went out and only a small red lamp remained burning near the medium. With the aid of loud classical music played on a cassette recorder, Luiz went into a deep trance and began talking to the great painters. Quick as lightning he squeezed colours from a great number of tubes and started painting. The drawings took about three minutes each and the oil paintings about five. One could have heard a pin drop in the hall throughout the entire demonstration. When the séance was over and Luiz had come out of his trance all the pictures were hung on the wall or otherwise displayed and I was allowed to photograph them.

My extraordinary meeting with the healer, psychic surgeon and natural scientist, Lourival de Freitas

I waited three weeks for this unusual meeting which an intermediary had arranged for me. It was to have lasted half-an-hour and ended up lasting three hours! When I entered his home in Rio de Janeiro he welcomed me with a typical Brazilian *cafezinho*. My arrival coincided with that of a general accompanied by his wife and daughter. The daughter, whom Lourival had cured of breast cancer, brought X-ray pictures and the results of blood tests with her. She had been discharged by her doctors as cured and she brought Lourival her doctors' greetings. Overjoyed, she flung her arms around Lourival's neck. He took us both into another room and showed me the girl's breasts, permitting me to take photographs.

The following report for inclusion in this book was signed and approved personally by Lourival:

"The healer and natural scientist, Lourival de Freitas, has long enjoyed world fame. His paranormal powers also aroused great interest in Europe during the many years he spent there, especially in England where he submitted to all manner of scientific experiment. He works almost always in close co-operation with well-known doctors in that he asks his patients, particularly those suffering from cancer, for their medical documents such as X-rays, laboratory analyses, diagnoses etc. After examining these documents he intervenes when classical medicine has declared the case beyond hope. He either performs psychic surgery which lasts only a few minutes and is carried out without anaesthetic or he uses plant products which he prepares from sponges, roots, herbs etc. collected in the Amazon region. These cure cancer and other "incurable" diseases in the shortest possible time. Only then do the doctors intervene anew to confirm by fresh laboratory tests, blood analyses and X-rays that the patient is cured. In very exceptional cases where classical medicine has long since given up all hope, Lourival uses his paranormal abilities to perform psychic surgery lasting a few seconds during which he removes the malignant tumour or kidney stone or other cause of disease from the patient's body without any incision, before the eyes of all those present, simply by pressing on a crystal glass.

"In cases such as these he also asks the person he has healed to submit to all the medical examinations necessary officially to confirm by all the scientific means available to classical medicine that the disease has, in fact, disappeared.

"Thus, Lourival is without doubt a most exceptional healer whose principle it is to accept no payment for his healing activity. For this reason he lives in the most frugal way possible with his wife and his three-year-old daughter. A remarkable circumstance is that Lourival operates only when he feels drawn, so to speak, to a patient, that is to say when he feels that precisely this person should be healed by him. It is therefore not sufficient merely to ask him for healing; Lourival himself must decide which sickness he can and should heal. He promises no one that they shall be cured but endeavours to heal in accordance with his own particular code of ethics."

After the general and his wife and daughter had left we sat at the table for a long time avidly exchanging ideas and experience. Lourival showed me all the roots he had collected in Amazonia, often digging them up from depths of ten metres in the ground. The army was always available to help him with his "excavations". He frequently disappears in Amazonia for as much as three months at a time, rather as the Filipino psychic surgeons withdraw to their caves to recharge their batteries, so to speak. Lourival took up his guitar and played me several lovely songs, singing them in a gentle, pleasing voice. One of these was a love song dedicated to his wife in which he paid her the most beautiful compliments a husband can find. She had borne him a child just three weeks previously and he tended this baby as though it were a fragile flower. I was deeply touched and filled with joy by this unique encounter.

Healing meditation plus individual treatment

Experience obtained during the healing meditation sessions I hold at my house every week-end for groups of 20-30 persons or in halls and churches for between 80 and 400 people—patients and their relatives and others seeking help—has shown a great increase in awareness among people of all ages. These sessions afford an inner delight in and a positive attitude towards life, a deepening of faith (irrespective of confession since meditation is done on an ecumenical basis) and a new conception of health and perfection. In 1983 and 1984 I ran these sessions together with individual therapy voluntarily and as an experiment each week-end for the International Creative Centre of the Foundation for the Promotion of Juvenile and Adult Education, the "Wasserfallenhof Academy" in Reigoldswil, Canton Baselland in Switzerland.

My condition was that all healing meditation and individual therapy take place at my house since it is there that I achieve the best vibrations and where I feel most secure and protected. All voluntary donations went towards juvenile and adult education at the International Creative Centre. The lectures and healing meditation sessions held in halls and churches took place in Lenzburg, Liestal and Wald in Switzerland and in Goslar in Germany during an Easter symposium and also on the Philippines. Patients from different countries and of various races and confessions came to these sessions as the result of recommendations. No meditation is ever undertaken before the body, soul and spirit have been cleansed. Each participant must first of all set aside all hate, rancour and injustice, must free himself from the error of his ways and direct his thoughts towards health and perfection. Each one must become aware that the power of spiritual self-healing exists in each and every one of us. Each one must silently forgive himself and all others who might have caused him spiritual injury, since to hurt is tantamount to making sick. We consign all this to the violet flame that consumes all suffering, problems and cares. Thus, everyone has to hand the "ignition switch" by means of which he can trigger his own healing. We sit up straight but relaxed, legs slightly apart, hands in our laps, palms upwards; we close our eyes and let ourselves go. We take three deep breaths—in . . . out.

I intone an introductory prayer, "Come, Holy Spirit, fill the hearts of all here present and light in us the fire of your Divine love. You who have gathered together the people of all tongues, Eternal Father, grant us the grace of the presence here among us of the Holy Spirit, to enlighten us, to teach us all truth, strengthen us in all goodness, guard against all evil and comfort us in all adversity, through Christ our Lord, Amen." Then I start singing, imagining the vibration of waves of love, and we all sing the OM together. OM means Amen (so be it) and is the invocation of the Holy Spirit, the Divine creative power that builds up the whole created structure of vibrations. This also stimulates the higher centres of power and light (Chakras) in our heads. We allow ourselves to be carried by the music accompanying our meditation and swung up to a higher level of consciousness. We become positively aware of ourselves and, for three-quarters of an hour, we journey together towards perfection. The important thing is to know that we carry God within us as the source of love, truth and security; that, by turning towards the light in deep meditation, a great, widened path of light is created which serves as a channel via which we acquire the knowledge, intuition and wisdom we so urgently need if we are to make constant spiritual progress. During these healing meditation sessions we awáken and activate our own inner powers of healing by setting our egos aside, letting ourselves go and yielding completely to our souls. We feel Divine energy vitalizing our life stream, pulsing through us with healing power and renewing and reshaping us from within. We become aware of healthy cells taking over from the sick ones, thus restoring health to body, soul and spirit. We strive after the rhythms of harmony and perfection and fall into accord with Nature, the universe and our Creator, letting His will be done. In conclusion we join hands and, together, send light, love, strength and peace out into the world. Then, once again, we sing the OM three times, take three deep breaths (in . . . out . . .) and feel the OM filling us with Divine strength.

My lectures about the spiritual healers in the Philippines

When I first went to the Philippines I never imagined I should one day give lectures or, indeed, write a book about this country and its people. But inspiration was so strong that my immediate reaction was to pass on the knowledge and experience I had acquired; that is to say, it simply happened. The first lectures about spiritual healing and psychic surgery, which I always gave in conjunction with a session of healing meditation, took place at a time when a great deal of negative opinion was appearing in the Press and on television with the result that serious doubt was sown in the minds of many readers and viewers.

However, deep inside me I was convinced that, one day, good would triumph over evil. In the meantime those people who were not then sufficiently mature to understand God's work have learnt a thing or two. The crowded halls confirm the tremendous interest that exists. One lady journalist wrote in a newspaper, "That was a test of courage which Madeleine Riedel-Michel passed with flying colours from start to finish."

I was invited to attend the opening of the "International Creative Centre of the Foundation for the Promotion of Juvenile and Adult Education". The famous philosopher, Dr. Hans Endres, asked me to go to Northern Germany to an Easter symposium organized by the "Society for Universal Prevention and Regeneration" in Goslar, aimed at promoting the care of psycho-physical health. There I made the acquaintance of the scientist, Dr. W. A. Frank, and many other interesting people active in the sphere of healing and life reform. There were many interesting exchanges of ideas and experience and mutual inspiration was stimulating. After that I received many invitations to give lectures at all sorts of institutions. However, I preferred not to dissipate my energies but rather to concentrate them on communicating my experiences only to those enlightened people who were ready and mature enough to profit from them. But the time will come when doctors, nurses and therapists will start to take an interest and then I shall also be prepared to lecture at hospitals.

II. Fundamentals

Spiritual and Intellectual Powers

1. The Power of Thought

We Europeans must first learn to think properly and positively unless, of course, we were fortunate enough to have this ability given us at birth and encouraged throughout our early years by positively-thinking parents. Our affluence here in the Western world and the resulting stress phenomena at college and university, at work and in our private lives, together with the negative influences of radio, television and the Press to which we and our children are exposed day in and day out, give rise to unnecessary anxiety and desires in roughly equal parts. If our thinking were positive and we ourselves radiantly aware of God's love and protection, we should be subject to far fewer diseases.

Negative thinking opens wide the door to cancer for we must never forget that thought is a force that can damage body and soul and even destroy them. Not only does it disrupt the organism—blood circulation, heart, lungs, stomach, digestion and the entire nervous system—it also upsets the harmony of family and social life.

Your way of thinking determines your disposition and physical condition

I know three people who attracted the dreaded disease of cancer like magnets by the years they spent in unabatable fear of it.

When the doctor finally confirmed that they had, in fact, developed the disease they were quite literally overjoyed for now they could go around telling everyone they had cancer. Everyone felt sorry for them with the result that, at last, people were taking sufficient notice of them.

They nurtured their cancers as a mother her child until the dreadful truth suddenly dawned upon them. It is usually possible to help people such as these only just before they die since they refuse to see clearly until it is almost too late. But then, when their guilt complexes, their feelings of vengeance and rancour have encompassed their self-destruction, they succeed in setting them aside so that at least they may be received into God's all-merciful arms.

Avoid whenever you can all those who constantly transmit negative thoughts, those who are full of hate, envy, egoism, dissatisfaction, criticism, tyranny and jealousy, those who express themselves only in terms of pessimism, lament and cynicism. They create a paralyzing, depressing and claustrophobic atmosphere calculated to foster disease. Their negative vibrations can entirely poison the premises you share with them.

Always remember—no matter how well-intentioned you may be, *you* cannot change these people; their egoism has so ensnared them in spiritual blindness that it is only some catalytic enlightenment which might one day show them that *they can change themselves*. All you can do is pray that this will soon come about and patiently send them enlightening thoughts.

"Do not conform any longer to the pattern of this world, but be transformed by the renewing of your mind. Then you will be able to test and approve what God's will is—his good, pleasing and perfect will. *Romans*, 12:2 (New International Version)

If you wish to nurture positive, even healing thoughts, you must do everything in your power to achieve harmony of body, soul and spirit. That is to say, you must cease your constant nagging, criticising and condemning. Seek, rather, to think healing and loving thoughts which are vital for your increasing welfare and the prosperity of your family.

If you are ill, you would do well not to address your thoughts to sickness but to stress the word health in all you think, speak and do. This word will prove to be your salvation.

Try, also, to invest your home with great love and a bouyant atmosphere for in it your whole self is mirrored. Light a candle occasionally to afford the rooms brightness. Radiate positiveness, starting with your very first thought each morning, in that you send a prayer of gratitude heavenwards. Carry these positive emanations with you as you go from one room of your home to another.

I have discovered that the more people meditate in my home, the stronger and more illuminating the vibrations that flow through its rooms become and the better, happier and more secure my visitors feel.

Always remember—what you make of your thoughts, your emanation, your feelings and your home is entirely up to you. It depends only on you whether you accept life positively and whether you are prepared to allow goodness, happiness and love to flourish within you.

Exercise

I have faith in myself. I affirm the good in myself. My thoughts are pure. I radiate love on all my fellow men. I am positive and full of light.

2. The Power of Speech

Jesus said that, on the day of reckoning, each of us will have to account for every wrong-minded word we have ever spoken.

A word spoken positively can completely heal since constructive, health-oriented and revitalizing words create a harmonious field of vibrations which surrounds you for a long time, warming your soul and uplifting it.

"When he (Jesus) came down from the mountainside, large crowds followed him. A man with leprosy came and knelt before him and said, 'Lord, if you are willing, you can make me clean.'

Jesus reached out his hand and touched the man. 'I am willing,' he said. 'Be clean!' Immediately he was cured of his leprosy." *Matthew* 1:1-4 (New International Version)

Doctors and healers know that the power of the positive word can even accomplish spontaneous healing. But we also know that negative words can cause sickness and spiritual distress.

Hurtful words of this kind are spoken in the course of day-to-day living more often than we are, perhaps, prepared to admit; I am particularly anxious to enlighten my readers on this score. The following maxim should help you to moderate your words in future:

Every word you speak comes home to roost!

Everyone wants to lead a pleasant, cheerful life, to be welcome among a wide circle of friends and good acquaintances and to enjoy harmonious communication with them.

The table given below is intended to help you in everyday life and social intercourse.

The following kinds of word generate a positive field of vibrations:

encouraging	vitalizing
strengthening	warming
stimulating	cheerful
powerful	uplifting
life-imbueing	conciliatory

The following kinds of word generate a negative field of vibrations:

criticizing	reproachful
discourteous	condemning
irritating	self-willed
malicious	fault-finding
hurtful	disparaging

The consequences of negative words:

Discourteous words can cause	hardening of the blood vessels, circulatory malfunctions, disturbances of the liver and the eyesight.
Constant criticism and fault-finding can cause	rheumatism, cramped muscles, inflamation of the joints and muscles, bone dehydration; also encourages cardiac infarctus.
Complaining and self-willed words can cause	colds and bronchial diseases, nervous malfunction of the thyroid, palpitation and high blood pressure, goitre, proud flesh, pneumonia and even the necessity of surgical operations.
Repressive and tyrannical words can cause	asthma, constriction, cramp of all kinds.

Many readers will already have discovered for themselves that a negative word can paralyze and destroy. It can thrust an unstable or highly-strung person into an abyss of darkest depression from which he will emerge—if at all—only with specialized aid. I have known many women whose tyranny and constant nagging of their husbands, whose dissatisfaction in marriage and whose negative manner of speech towards their husbands have made of these men psychic and physical wrecks. They were no longer able to laugh and because they laughed no more they became sick. Once confined to their beds, they were even more at the mercy of their wives who, secretly, even desired the death of their partners. These marriages eventually ended in divorce since the situation became intolerable for all concerned and the women had no intention of changing their ways. If they had been prepared to do so, divorce could perhaps have been avoided.

Today these men have changed beyond recognition. Years of psychic and medical care have succeeded in restoring their self-confidence and their personalities have reburgeoned.

Those whom have remarried sought for their second attempt a sunny-natured woman with whom they could be happy and have equally warm-natured children. I have, of course, also known cases where it was the man who made his wife's life sheer hell. I have cited these examples as a warning to watch our words more carefully in day-to-day living, to utter only light-bringing, strengthening and reconciling words in our daily contacts—words that strengthen the positive field of vibrations, that encourage and revitalize us, that warm our hearts and souls and incite us to give of our utmost.

I should like to close this chapter with a quotation from the *Wisdom of Solomon*, 7:15-17:

"God hath granted me to speak as I would, and to conceive as is meet for the things that are given me: because it is he that leadeth unto wisdom, and directeth the wise.

For in his hands are both we and our words; all wisdom also and knowledge of workmanship.

For he hath given me certain knowledge of the things that are, namely, to know how the world was made, and the operation of the elements." (Apocrypha)

Exercise

I speak to all those about me clear and encouraging words. I transmit great warmheartedness. Harmony, light, love and strength accompany my words.

3. The Power of Faith

The power of faith affords us the roots, the rock-like foundations, the steadfastness and the perseverance life demands of us. Where is this better described than in the Bible which explains to us, in the *First Epistle General of Peter*, 1:5-19 (New International Version), the aim of faith and the path thereto:

. . . for you "Who through faith are shielded by God's power until the coming of the salvation that is ready to be revealed in the last time. In this you greatly rejoice, though now for a little while you may have had to suffer grief in all kinds of trials. These have come so that your faith—of greater worth than gold, which perishes even though refined by fire—may be proved genuine and may result in praise, glory and honour when Jesus Christ is revealed. Though you have not seen him, you love him; and even though you do not see him now, you believe in him and are filled with an inexpressible and glorious joy, for you are receiving the goal of your faith, the salvation of your souls."

And in his *Epistle to the Hebrews*, 11:1,3 and 6 (New International Version) Paul writes, "Now faith is being sure of what we hope for and certain of what we do not see. By faith we understand that the universe was formed at God's command, so that what is seen was not made out of what was visible.

"And without faith it is impossible to please God, because anyone that comes to him must believe that he exists and that he rewards those who earnestly seek him."

I have prayed and meditated with many people of all manner of confessions, wherever I happened to be, in South America, Europe, Thailand, India, Nepal or the Philippines. Wherever I prayed and meditated I was aware of the depth of these people's faith and the extent of their love; and together we sent light out into the world and formed a source of harmony.

It is my belief that the time has come for mankind to pursue ecumenical unity far more purposefully and to realize that it is wrong to condemn those whose beliefs differ from our own, to ridicule them or—far worse—to suppress them. We have no right whatever to do any of these things. We should do far better to remember that we can attain the goal of faith only by our willingness to live in harmony for and with one another, giving and understanding and dedicating ourselves unreservedly to our Creator. When your faith is such that you are at one with God, you hold the key to happiness in your hands.

Exercise

I am a child of God. He protects me wherever I go. I have confidence in myself and in my fellowmen. I believe that God is working mightily in and through me. I believe there is a perfect solution to every difficult situation in my life. God is all-powerful. I feel his strength flowing through me. My faith makes me free, strong and perfect.

4. The Power of Prayer

I should like to share with you my favourite prayer, the one I say each day before starting work. It expresses true humility in the most wonderful, profound and devoted way. It enables us to put our egos entirely aside and requires us to give ourselves completely to God and our fellowmen; it incites us to fresh endeavour and greater cheerfulness, of which we all stand in urgent need.

The Prayer of St. Francis of Assisi

> O Lord make me an instrument of Thy peace;
> Where there is hatred, let me put love;
> Where there is resentment, let me put forgiveness;
> Where there is discord, let me put unity;
> Where there is doubt, let me put faith;
> Where there is error, let me put truth;
> Where there is despair, let me bring happiness;
> Where there is sadness, let me bring joy;
> Where there is darkness, let me bring light.
> O Master grant that I may desire rather:
> To console than to be consoled.
> To understand rather than to be understood.
> To love rather than to be loved.
> Because it is in giving that we receive;
> In forgiving that we obtain forgiveness;
> In dying that we rise to eternal life.

> Amen.

Every prayer we pray, in no matter what situation, always affords us divine protection and guidance. The only condition is that it come from an honest and sincere heart. I would therefore suggest that, every morning when you waken, you put yourself prayerfully into God's hands and say short prayers at intervals throughout the day. Put aside your feelings of guilt and cease to torture yourself. Remember that God is good and that He forgives even the blackest sinner. Ask for forgiveness and repent your misdeeds, reconcile yourself with all those from whom you are in any way estranged: this is necessary if your prayers are to be answered. But nothing can be gained by insistence—you can do no more than wait upon God and allow things to take their course. God has time and He alone knows why He keeps us waiting, first subjecting us to tests. You would do well to include the following sentence in your prayers:

"Not my will, O Lord, but Thy will be done."

Remember one thing—God never forsakes us, never leaves us alone in any situation, no matter how black things sometimes look; for we are His children and He loves us with all His heart. Many people have admitted to me that they turn to God only in moments of dire distress. During the time I was working with the psychic surgeon, Josephine Sison, in the Philippines I saw terrible situations of this kind. After their introduction to spiritual healing and psychic surgery and the subsequent sessions of prayer and treatment, and also after psychic surgery, severely shaken people often asked me, "Did I have to pass through such a serious illness before realizing, before feeling just how strong the power of prayer can be? Here I have been permitted to learn the significance of prayer. I have only now learned that God loves me. I have been healed by the power of faith and prayer will be my most constant companion."

The last wish of a man suffering from cancer, with advanced metastases and only a short time to live, was to visit the healers on the Philippines. He said to me, "The power of prayer that I have experienced here and the deep faith have convinced me that I can now die in peace." He died two months later, gratefully surrendering himself to God.

These people have come to understand that the only prayers that are answered are those uttered in deep faith from a pure and sincere heart; that God gives each of us the chance of believing in him, of recognizing and loving him, even if we do so only a short time before we die.

In conclusion I should like to give my readers a petitionary prayer that I say several times each day while I am working:

"God grant me the strength to see each day through and to come a small step closer to you on the way. Grant that I may transmit to my patients the great strength you give me, since all they desire is health and the healing of body, soul and spirit."

5. The Power of Gratitude

"I desire to do your will, O my God; your law is within my heart." *Psalm* 40:8.

There are people who think little or not at all about gratitude since they are interested only in bolstering their own egos until the day when a serious illness forces them into hospital. It is then that they realize for the first time how helpless they are and how dependent upon other people. Their first grateful glance is given the nurse who looks after them. They start thinking about the lives they lead. Below is an example that I experienced at close range.

A man who had been unfaithful to his wife on very many occasions suddenly contracted cancer of the testicles and was taken to hospital. His condition was very serious. His wife, whom he regarded more or less as part of the furniture, the mother of his children who had for years kept his house in order but whom he refused to see as a loved companion, stood by him through thick and thin, nursed him and showed him how much she loved him and how anxious his illness made her. He was very surprised at her reaction. At first he was overwhelmed by a sense of guilt but then he suddenly saw clearly. He was aware of great gratitude to God for his sickness; he repented, turned over a new leaf and discovered a new and unusual love for his wife which, to the astonishment of his doctors, caused him to be completely cured. From the depths of his gratitude he had recognized the risk he was running, grabbing the chance offered him by completely changing his way of life and his attitude towards it. Many years have passed since then. He overcame his cancer and now enjoys a happy marriage.

In *Psalm* 146:2 (New International Version) you will find a song of praise to God:

"Praise the Lord, O my soul.

I will praise the Lord all my life,

I will sing praise to my God as long as I live."

Praise God whenever you are able. Let your heart and your soul speak through your praise and sing as much as you can, whenever the opportunity presents itself. Singing makes you happy and generates positive vibrations all about you—a wonderful field of force.

Late in the quiet of the evening on 5th April, 1984 I wrote this poem:

> Gratitude
> Grateful for this simple life
> Here in the mountains and caves.
> Grateful and in deepest awe
> I owe you humility and praise.
> Gratefully I welcome all the people
> You send me O Lord.
> Gratefully I alleviate their pain
> Knowing that Thy will be done.
> Gratefully I draw the strength of Love
> From the wells of Heaven.
> Gratefully I send out my life's strength
> Through the channel of joy.
> Gratefully and profoundly at peace
> I am at one with all my dear ones.

Let us surrender more and more to gratitude. Send a prayer of thanks heavenwards before you think, speak and act. Before starting work, when you are with your family, before and after meals, before visitors come to see you, when you are confronted with a difficult task.

Open the gates of gratitude within you and let love and strength flow out to your fellowmen through the thus widened spiritual channel.

Exercise

I am grateful for all the love I am privileged to give and to receive. In deepest gratitude I bow before you, O Lord, accepting my life gladly. Your joy is my joy and you fill my whole life.

6. The Power of Love

When I began writing this book in the Philippines on 28th March, 1984, where I was surrounded by such lovable, natural and sincere people, I knew from the start that I should be writing a long chapter about love. I felt myself spiritually linked with the lovers, the married couples and the children but, spiritually, I also experienced how love could be suffocated by jealousy and what the consequences could be. I have never ceased to believe in love and it means a very great deal to me. For this reason I should like to begin this passage with the most beautiful lovesong that even the Bible contains—*Solomon's Song of Songs*. In one series of verses he praises the love between a man and a woman who become one and then lose each other, who seek and then find each other:

"Let him kiss me with the kisses of his mouth—for your love is more delightful than wine." (1:2)

"How beautiful your sandalled feet, O prince's daughter! Your graceful legs are like jewels, the work of a craftsman's hands. Your navel is a rounded goblet that never lacks blended wine. Your waist is a mound of wheat encircled by lilies.

Your breasts are like two fawns, twins of a gazelle.

Your neck is like an ivory tower.

Your eyes are the pools of Hesbon by the gate of Bathrabbim.

Your nose is like the tower of Lebanon looking towards Damascus. Your head crowns you like Mount Carmel.

Your hair is like royal tapestry; the king is held captive by its tresses. How beautiful you are and how pleasing, O love, with your delights!

Your stature is like that of the palm, and your breasts like clusters of fruit." (7:1-8)

"His left arm is under my head and his right arm embraces me.

Daughters of Jerusalem, I charge you, Do not arouse or awaken love until it so desires." (8:3-7)

It is the power of love symbolically expressed here to which I wish to draw your attention and I should like to recommend that you read *Solomon's Song of Songs* now and again, that you think about it and that you even read it aloud to your spouse. In this way you can both recall the time when love was young and perhaps rekindle it. You should continually rediscover each other. When you think about love you must realize that thoughts of this kind make you joyful and this causes a positive chemical process in your body which, in turn, leads to a constructive attitude which generates health. Your spirit and your soul are borne on wings of harmony and health.

During my work I have been privileged to see how powerful love can be when lovers are separated and love has grown strong in spite of the oceans that lie between, when lovers have found each other in spite of the opposition of family and friends, in spite of problems of race and creed, and have experienced true and fruitful love. That is why I agree with my favourite poet, Zenta Maurina, when she writes as follows about love:

"Love is the ultimate magic when it has been transfigured, illumined and consolidated by friendship."

Partnership

Love may not be self-willed, domineering and possessive. Genuine love equalizes, bears you up, harmonizes, releases you and incites you to give of your utmost. If this is not the case and if love tends more to drag you down then there is something wrong with the way you think and feel and you will have to make a great many changes. Love must be tended and nurtured. I imagine it always as a plant in full bloom that must be watered regularly lest it wilt and then die of hunger and thirst. And if you talk gently to the fragile soul of the flower it will be grateful and live much longer. It is exactly the same with love. If you are discontented with your partner, it is high time to do some spiritual accounting and to make some changes in yourself. You wanted to shape your partner according to your own lights and this has resulted in coercion, disharmony and a generally stifling atmosphere. If you try to keep your partner against his or her will, you will only cause both of you unhappiness. True and selfless love is characterized by humility, renunciation and devotion and a capacity to forgive.

Dr. Beat Imhof always stresses in his lectures that it is as the Italians phrase it—"Ti voglio bene"—I wish you well. Thus love is mainly an affair of give and take. We all know that nagging and complaining is calculated to poison any relationship.

She often thinks: If only he were more self-assured, more successful; he disappoints me. If only he were more tender, more romantic, attentive and kind, we could be so happy.

And he thinks: If only she understood me better when I come home and tell her about the worries at work. Instead of understanding, all I hear is nagging, reproaches and complaints about the children I love so much. I would give anything for a little loving attention but she constantly keeps me at a distance.

Where is the root of these difficulties?

Both partners expect too much of the other and are inevitably always being disappointed. Both have forgotten that each must first start generating a loving, partner-oriented atmosphere before any demands may be made upon the other. A radical change in both partners' thinking is essential here. For example:

Women must first realize that men think and act in a way totally different from their own. Here is the circle I draw for a man: ⊘ profession/work.

Three-quarters of this circle are devoted entirely to his job, i.e. to the objectively concrete. The other quarter is divided between his hobbies, his family, his on-training etc.

And now the circle for a woman: ⊘ family.

A man must learn to understand that three-quarters of this circle belong to the family, to husband, children and household, i.e. the subjectively human. When the opportunity presents itself and the children are bigger, a woman can devote some of this time to her hobbies or part-time work.

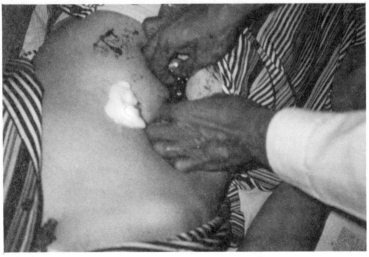

"Medium Operador" Virgilio Gutierrez, Manila, performing a mediumistic operation in 1984.

You have to accept the fact that men and women are spiritually and physically different. Men and women will always remain complete enigmas to each other—but that is what makes the whole thing so fascinating! It encourages us constantly to rediscover each other.

On the basis of many years of experience I should like to give both partners some advice and to suggest a few exercises.

For her: When your partner comes home discouraged and depressed do not make matters worse but try to imbue him with positive thoughts. Encourage him, put your arms around him, accept him the way he is and help him to be strong and courageous. And never ask too much of him. Talk about the children later, when the worst of his tiredness has passed. He needs time to switch off and to switch over. Cook him something tasty for supper—since love is said to be closely connected with the stomach. Spoil him and devote yourself to him selflessly in all respects including the sexual, since here in particular he obtains the reassurance he so badly needs. Give your imagination free rein, for the more cheerful you are, the more compliments you pay him, the more he will love you and you will thus become an indispensable source of strength for him. Help him in every situation that arises and stand by him. Leave him sufficient elbow-room for his professional development and practise generous and tolerant thinking in every situation. Forgive him whenever there is the need for forgiveness.

Pray for him daily: I send you light, love, strength and understanding. Peace, harmony and happiness pervade our home for we love one another, we are one and nothing can part us.

For him: Learn to understand your partner's sensitive soul and take an interest in the little things that are of importance to her even if they appear insignificant to you. Feel for and with her. Endeavour to see in her an angel that emanates peace, security and love. If you wish all this repeatedly, your thoughts will be mirrored in her. Help her with the children's education so that she does not feel alone in this for nothing is more difficult than the upbringing of the young. Discuss with her the problems posed by the children. Try to reveal your wishes to her after having held her in your arms tenderly so that she is aware of the security you afford her. Constantly rediscover your wife. Bring her a little gift from time to time—give her a flower, write her a few loving words, treat her to a romantic evening somewhere pleasant. Give her a great deal of tenderness so that she knows always that she can cling to you. In every situation let her be your lover, the mother of your children and your wife. Give her your entire confidence and forgive her whenever there is anything to forgive. Make sure that all your quarrels end in perfect reconciliation.

Pray for her daily: We are light, love and strength and dwell together in harmony. We love each other, we understand each other better as time goes on. We are one and nothing can part us.

How to overcome jealousy

There is a German play on words which has it that jealousy is an obsession that passionately seeks whatever can cause suffering. Jealousy does not bind the loved one to you but repels him—or her, ultimately precipitating him into precisely what you were endeavouring, with lurking violence, to avoid. The negative thoughts inspired by your jealousy awaken in your partner a sense of dissatisfaction, of a lack of liberty, even of enslavement. You can overcome your jealousy by daily spiritual discipline in the course of which you become aware that love does not mean domination. You must also realize that, whenever you suffer, it is always your ego that suffers. It is your ego that is disappointed, hurt, deceived and neglected. Set aside your self-pity and brooding, your feeling of being neglected and lost, your distrust and your possessiveness. Be assured that the more you meet your partner half-way and accord him confidence, attend to his wishes, affirm your oneness with him and avoid everything that could disrupt or jeopardize your partnership, the greater will be your gain. And if custom dictates that I write "him", it is understood that this also means "her". Try each day, in prayer and meditation in a quiet place, to send your partner light, love and strength. Be grateful that you have found each other and you will be surprised how much unsolicited affection you will receive. Once you have renounced your ego a delightful twoness will be opened to you and you will start to become aware of what lies behind everyday things. In this way you will experience the wealth and the joy of your existence as you had never done before.

The possessiveness of parents who frantically clutch their children to them, refusing to let them go their own way, is every bit as bad as jealousy within a partnership. When my own children started to be grown up and the time came for me to think about letting them go, when the first anxious thoughts obtruded about the harsh world into which I should soon be called to release them, I was glad to have the example of someone I trusted. I immediately recalled how my own parents had succeeded in launching all of us as grown children. Instead of showing anxiety they had sent us forth with trust in God. So I did the same as my own children went their various ways and have been doing so ever since.

Try to set your fears aside for your anxiety will be transmitted to your child and the consequences will be behavioural and health problems of all kinds: difficulties at school, inability to concentrate, disharmony, inability to cope with life and susceptibility to disease. Neither should you suffocate your children with a surfeit of maternal affection since this will force them into the defensive; they will protest and be forced to break out of the "gilded cage" in which you have imprisoned them lest they perish. Do not demand too much of them, subject them to undue pressure or confine them too closely since this can even cause diseases of the heart and lungs extending as far as asthma. On the other hand, do not make undue sacrifices for them either but let your children grow and prosper in liberty. Give them the chance of developing within the context of their own lives which will necessarily differ from yours.

In *The Prophet* Kahlil Gibran writes so beautifully:

"Your children are not your children.
They are the sons and daughters of Life's longing for itself.
They come through you but not from you, And though they are with you yet they belong not to you.

You may give them your love but not your thoughts,
For they have their own thoughts.
You may house their bodies but not their souls, For their souls dwell in the house of to-morrow,
Which you cannot visit, not even in your dreams.
You may strive to be like them, but seek not to make them like you.
For life goes not backward nor tarries with yesterday.
You are the bows from which your children as living arrows are sent forth.

The Archer sees the mark upon the path of the infinite, and
He bends you with His might that His arrows go swift and far.
Let your bending in the Archer's hand be for gladness;
For even as He loves the arrow that flies, so He loves also the bow that
is stable."

A prayer for the children:

I let my children go. I entrust their destiny to Your mercy, O Lord.
Grant them daily Your Divine protection and guidance in all they
think, speak and do. Grant that I may always be in the background as a
good mother—a reliable father, there whenever they need me.

The Healing Process as a Learning Process

You will enjoy this poem by Christian Morgenstern—it is one that
accompanied me along the way. It stresses the patience we should
practise every day:

> All is yielding and fulfilling.
> Just be patient and you'll see
> How your happiness will grow
> And, as the corn, garnish the fields,
> Until one day you smell the scent
> Of the richly ripened grain.
> Go forth, then, to your harvest
> And garner it into some deep place.

All periods of suffering are testing times and every healing process is
a process of learning imposed upon us by God so that we contemplate
our lives and bring our affirmation of our human condition to
perfection. In the *First Epistle of James* (5:15) it is written, "And the
prayer offered in faith will make the sick person well; the Lord will raise
him up. If he has sinned, he will be forgiven."

Have confidence in yourself and your spiritual powers of healing.
God will understand you in every situation for His goodness is far
greater than you realize. Always remember that each one of us has the
key to his healing in his own hand. All you have to do is await the
moment when your spirit grants this enlightenment. Then open the

shuttered windows of your darkened consciousness and let the sun of true perception shine upon your soul and the healing flow of vital strength flood your body. If necessary, obtain help at first from a healer or a doctor since they both know that it is not they that can heal you but you yourself, that is to say, God in you. The doctor and the healer serve merely as intermediaries. For this reason your direct link with God will later on suffice, the link you will find in prayer and meditation. You could even seek out a meditation group in your vicinity for these are becoming more and more numerous throughout the world, among all the confessions. Group meditation will expand your consciousness and you will feel yourself buoyed up and understood by people of like mind. Everything that at first you tolerated and suffered and then overcame in that you were granted enlightenment and revelation will become an important milestone in your life. Once you are restored to health you will have greater understanding for your suffering fellow men and women and your loving and sunny disposition will in turn serve them as a signpost to spiritual self-help.

Exercise:

I have confidence in myself and in the Divine healing powers within me. I am capable of renewing my spirit, my soul and my body from within. As a child of God I am filled with love and light, with spiritual clarity and optimism.

When you are sick, practise this exercise daily until you are restored to health. Let God work in you.

Obstacles in the Path of Healing

Should you meet someone who arrogantly or disparagingly declares that this or that therapy, be it spiritual or classically medical, has helped him not at all, you can be sure that he has the wrong attitude, or that he suffers from a negative way of thinking and preferred to hide his true feelings from the doctor or the therapist rather than to confide in them. He was, of course, far too impatient, unbelieving and filled with doubts to have been able to accept the therapy positively because his soul was too immature for healing; because he shut himself up against the healing powers of our Creator and refused to let them flow in.

In *Matthew* 14—31 it is written, "Immediately Jesus reached out his hand and caught him. 'You of little faith,' he said, 'why did you doubt?'" (New International Version)

I know how long a path a suffering person must tread, often for many years, before he can completely open his heart and develop true confidence in God and, ultimately, in himself, even if he has the help of doctors and therapists. He will suddenly experience an awakening of his soul. This surprises him and he begins to understand that he was merely lacking the necessary patience and perseverance, or that he was misled by members of his family who had wrong expectations of healing and had thus caused the convalescent to waver in his positive attitude towards his therapy. When relatives behave like this they render the convalescent a grave disservice.

During a moment of quiet the sufferer will also ask himself what caused all these obstructions to healing. And if he pays attention to his guiding inner voice, he will find the answer.

Was it wrong-headedness, superficiality, egoism, domineeringness, unforgivingness, self-torture, feelings of guilt, stress, pressure, discord, aggression, envy, resentment, distrust, hate, fear, impatience, doubt, brooding, a mania for always being in the right or just an unwillingness to return to health?

Now you have been able to determine the "faulty switching" or barrier which is blocking your way to recovery. You have understood where to begin with your "spring cleaning" in order to achieve harmony of body, soul and spirit which alone will enable you to attain perfect health.

At this point I should like to impress on all families who have a suffering person in their midst that they should give them real support in the therapy they are undergoing and encourage them to have confidence in their doctor or healer. Avoid arousing inconstancy in them—their condition will already be making them unstable enough. Help them to regain their self-confidence. Find the necessary patience and look forward, not to death, but to life. On the other hand, when the hours upon life's clock have, in accordance with God's will, finally run out, do not resist the inevitable. Help your suffering relation in every situation for it is up to us to make ourselves available to one another in gladness and in grief. Never forget that a suffering person has a special need of deep and genuine affection; selfless love is the ultimate remedy available to us here on earth.

Exercise for the whole family:

We are confident that . . . (name) will recover. We are helping him/her to return to health and surrounding him/her with love and security. We are, however, not smothering him/her by our concern but are leaving him/her free to develop his/her personality in accordance with the will of God. We are all God's children. We love each other and stick together through thick and thin.

Say this exercise out loud every day; the strength of the word will make it doubly effective.

From weakness to strength and greater courage

When you are feeling very weak, empty and wretched it is high time to start getting used to the idea of obtaining new strength. I know from experience gained at the time of my paralysis how difficult it is at first to implement this idea. But do not just settle for self-pity since this will not get you any further. You will do far better slowly, step by step, to start working on yourself—daily, even hourly, in your lighter moments. And rejoice at the tiniest sign of progress!

A patient came to me suffering from deep depression. She told me anxiously, her features drawn and her eyes full of tears, "I can't go on—I won't go on. My husband and my children expect far too much of me and on top of that I am dreadfully jealous. I dread responsibility and refuse to do all the things I should do. I can't cook or cope with the housework anymore. Then I am overcome by feelings of guilt and want to make up for everything all at once. And then the prospect of it all paralyzes me anew and I yell at my husband and the children who, again, expect too much of me. I feel completely repressed and have no desire to live. The only thing that preoccupies me is the thought of death. I know that this is just another load that I am placing on the family but I just can't go on. It does what it wants with me."

This last remark was a reference by the patient to her autonomic nervous system which is not subject to the conscious will. This preoccupation with death was the most serious source of aggression against the patient herself; she was simply judging and executing herself.

These people are of particular importance to me and I spend a great deal of time in discussion with them and in praying for them. I strengthen their nervous systems and try to calm them. I offer them as much security and affection as I am able since their thinking is confused and erroneous. In the case of many of these patients I have seen how they have slowly come to accept life again, to see a ray of light in the depths of their souls and, step by step, to regain confidence in themselves until ultimately they recovered completely. In this way they found their way back to the unalloyed joy in living they had known as children.

Never say to a depressive person, "You've got to try", as that is precisely what they cannot do. The result is merely to discourage them further and create fresh obstructions.

Here are a few simple rules that experience has proved to be helpful. Just let things happen—let go. Relax. Have confidence in yourself and let God work in you. In your lighter moments, concentrate on the good in yourself for you are a child of God. Never forget that He loves you and that He wants you to be happy and satisfied. These thoughts of the security God offers will help you to build a foundation of strength and courage. You will have discovered that the sources of strength required to cope with life lie in quiet.

Exercise:

I let God work in me. God fills my soul with self-confidence. I am relaxed and receptive. I am healthy! I am strong! I am courageous! I can cope with life and am suddenly able to do things that demand of me enthusiasm and full commitment.

The acceptance of life

Before you set out upon this earthly path you were shown the life that lay ahead. There were the cares and the heartache, the misery and the suffering, the vices that would lay hold of you, the error that would imprison you. There was the sharp anger in which you would brood, the hate, the arrogance, the pride and the shame. But there was also the joy of each day full of light and dreams, where lament and vexation have no place and the source of all gifts runs. Where love grants the substance-clad the joyous intimation of release; where man once wrenched from human anguish thinks as one chosen by sublimer spirits. You were shown the evil and the good. You were shown the abundance of your faults. You were shown the wounds whence you would bleed. You were shown the helping-hand of angels. As you beheld the life that was to be you heard a voice that asked you if you dared accept that which awaited since the hour was soon to strike. And once again you weighed all that was bad and then declared in firm and ringing tones, "This is the life that I desire to live", and thus accepted all that lay ahead. Thus were you born into this realm of earth, thus you set out upon life's promised path. Lament not, therefore, when it fails to please—this life that, unborn, you had once accepted.

In a quiet moment ask yourself if you have accepted your life, your destiny as it is at present. Even if it seems to you to be disagreeable, unfair and pointless, rest assured that every destiny corresponds to God's plan and is entirely just. Never ask why such a hard fate should fall upon precisely you or your family; accept, rather, exactly that which hurts the most and learn through this to accept that which you would prefer to repulse. Stand fast against the primitive fears that threaten in the form of danger, enemies, worries, privations and disease. In *John* 14:27 you will read, "Do not let your hearts be troubled and do not be afraid."

If you accept things as they are, if you overcome, if you pass the hard test, you will recognize the truth and come to new awareness. Do not hate your enemy but send him thoughts of love, light and strength until one day—and even if it takes years—he sees the light and becomes your friend. Learn to love your fate and that of people close to you. Make a rich experience of pain as well and you will unfold like the rosebud that becomes a scented rose. By accepting life wholeheartedly at all ages you will develop the strength and the talents that slumber within you and you will be astounded how little you have previously used them and how forcefully you suddenly begin to rediscover your life. Do not look back and live gratefully each hour as it comes.

Exercise:

I am strength. I am absolutely capable of mastering my life. God is in and with me. I am never alone. I radiate happiness, harmony and love.

The 7 Energy Centres (Chakras) or the 12 Portals (Channels) that correspond in the Subtle Body to the Glandular and Nervous Systems of the Physical

When my father transmitted his vast knowledge of spiritual healing to me twenty-three years ago—at a time when we were total outsiders in regard to medicine—I knew the time would come when not only a chosen few would use this secret craft but that, in the approaching Age of Aquarius, spiritual awareness and maturity would also be achieved by doctors, therapists and healers. When this comes about these energy centres will be taken into greater consideration in diagnosis, the choice of treatment and its application. The patient, too, will learn in the course of his return to health to discover these spiritual, psychic and energy centres and, by regular spiritual exercise, to awaken and activate the healing powers slumbering within him and thus ultimately to attain perfect harmony of body, soul and spirit.

If you read *Revelations* 1-22, you will repeatedly come across the numbers 7 and 12 which are the symbolic reflection of the 7 original and the 12 expanded energy centres in the body (temple = body). *Revelations* reflects what is happening in the world:

7	12
7 Churches	12 Gates
7 Angles with the	12 Angels
7 Bowls holding the	12 Tribes of Israel
7 Last Plagues	12 Foundations
7 Golden Candlesticks	12 Apostles
7 Thunders symbolizing evil	12 Pearls
7 Trumpets	12 Stars
7 Seals	"The trees of life that bear fruit 12
7 Spirits of God	times, once every month."
7 Stars	

In the New Testament Jesus Christ, his 12 disciples and the 12 tribes of the children of Israel are linked with the energy centres that lie in our nervous and glandular systems. The prophets of old called them 12 cosmic centres and Paracelsus called them the 12 energy cores. They are the brightness in the spiritual heavens which demonstrate the workings of the spirit in the healing of the sick in that they reveal the light that shines throughout eternity while the dark night of materialism passes. You can keep these 12 energy centres constantly open, in balance and fresh by regular spiritual exercise. I shall be showing you some practical exercises that you can do every day, whether you be healthy, sick or convalescent. They will strengthen all your vital functions and contribute both to maintaining good health and to accelerating healing since the quantity of energy flowing through you will be increased. But first of all I must explain where these energy centres are situated, their significance and the colours (aura and emanation) in which the medium or the sensitive sees them. Here it must be borne in mind that every medium sees "his" or "her" own special colours.

The 7 Chakras
The 7 Sources of Spiritual Energy

This is the name given in the Far East to the energy centres in the subtle body that have as their counterparts in the physical body our glandular and nervous systems. Their location and significance are depicted in the following tables:

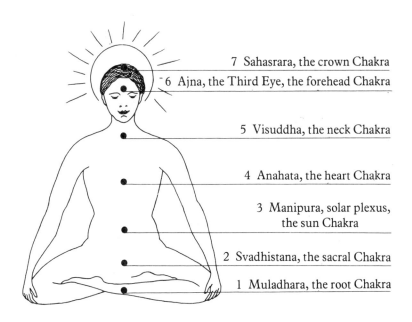

7 Sahasrara, the crown Chakra

6 Ajna, the Third Eye, the forehead Chakra

5 Visuddha, the neck Chakra

4 Anahata, the heart Chakra

3 Manipura, solar plexus, the sun Chakra

2 Svadhistana, the sacral Chakra

1 Muladhara, the root Chakra

The 12 Portals

In addition to the classical centres there are 5 others, so that we have a total of 12 portals (channels of spiritual strength), as my father explained to me:

In me there are:
Light, love, strength, wisdom, intuition, truth and knowledge

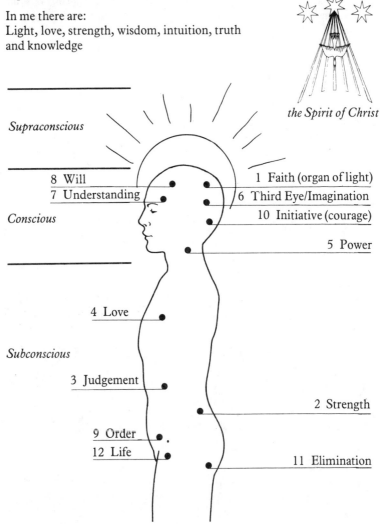

the Spirit of Christ

Supraconscious

8 Will

7 Understanding

1 Faith (organ of light)

6 Third Eye/Imagination

10 Initiative (courage)

Conscious

5 Power

4 Love

Subconscious

3 Judgement

2 Strength

9 Order

12 Life

11 Elimination

Your Subconscious

The energy centres attributed to the subconscious are: No. 2, Strength; No. 3, Judgement; No. 4, Love; No. 9, Order; No. 11, Elimination and No. 12, Life.

Negative experience in our contact with people, such as insults, injustice, disappointments, prejudice, aggression, bitter-sweet experiences in love, psychic shock and great agitation can mark the subconscious. Being subjected to pressure can cause palpitations, dragging pain, malfunction of the kidneys, liver, gall-bladder, stomach, intestines and digestion as well as general nervous dystonia (the subconscious is not called the "Dustbin of the Past" for nothing).

If you are suffering from any of these symptoms you would therefore do well finally and consciously to tidy up your past and get rid of all you have been suppressing, even if this has been going on for years and decades. You will experience a feeling of release.

This will cost you time and courage but it will be well worthwhile. Go and sit in a quiet corner and start writing. Make a list of all the people who have spiritually wounded you and arouse feelings of injustice in you—and don't be shy about it.

Write down your disappointments (in love and in other contexts); in this way you will air the feelings of agression that are still lurking within you. When you have finished writing light a fire in the grate, in the garden or wherever you can that enables you to be alone. Then read all the names three times out loud and say with the strength of the word:

"In the Name of Jesus Christ I forgive the person who has injured my soul. I love him (or her) with the love of Christ and he (or she) loves me with the love of Christ. Love heals both our spirits. We are liberated from all disharmony. We are at peace with one another from now on. God bless him (or her)."

Then ceremonially burn all you have written, for from this moment on you will have cleansed yourself and the subconscious of your enemy. Afterwards, when you encounter these people, you will be able to face them with strength, dignity and a cheerful heart.

Your Conscious

The energy centres attributed to the conscious are: No. 6,

Imagination; No. 5, Power; No. 7, Understanding; No. 8, Will; No. 10, Initiative.

Your conscious lies at the centre of your forehead and radiates to your five senses. Everything you consciously analyze, think and judge influences the spiritual powers located between forehead and throat. So do not be surprised if, shortly after thinking harshly critical or negative thoughts about someone, you start suffering from unhealthy symptoms in the region of the brain, forehead, eyes, ears, nose, mouth or throat.

Your Supraconscious

For purposes of observation and treatment it is your supraconscious that is of most interest to me and doubtless also to many healers and doctors. It is the crown centre, your organ of illumination, No. 1, Faith. This centre of illumination is activated, above all, in meditation, prayer and the unconditional acceptance of life. The results achieved are often astounding. It requires a great deal of time, regular exercise, patience and endurance to activate this highest centre. But it is particularly well worth doing. Your supraconscious is the crown of your life, the centre of all wisdom and intuition. In the course of (healing) meditation you can channel to all the other centres in your brain, body, nervous and glandular systems the energies and spiritual forces developed in this one. This vibration is for me the strongest, most beautiful and profound, the most fulfilling, devoted and successful in the Divine channel.

Where are these twelve energy centres (channels) located and what is their function?

If you want to discover quickly the reason for your sickness, the first thing you should do is consult the Table on page 66 in order to determine where the source of the trouble lies, in the conscious or the subconscious; in this way you will know where to tackle the problem of recovery. You can also thank your supraconscious when you start making spiritual progress. The main thing is to know that we exist on four different levels:
The substantial (the physical organism)
The etheric (the emotional)
The mental (the rational)

The spiritual (the veritable conscious = conscious being)

Each of these levels obtains and supplies energies from that dimension of the universe allotted it. When these wonderful vibrations flow from the higher to the lower dimensions (spiritual—mental—etheric—substantial) the person seeking aid experiences a sense of healing and well-being. We can activate these energies in the course of (healing) meditation, allowing them to flow through our receptive energy centres, and thus acquire powerful spiritualized vitality.

No. 1, The Energy Centre of Faith

The energy centre of faith lies in the middle of our foreheads (in the "golden centre") and "drives" the supraconscious. Its counterpart in the physical body is the pituitary gland. This energy centre is known as the organ of illumination or crown centre, also as the Thousand-leafed Lotus (vertex Chakra). No. 1 is our "supervisor" and the highest instance governing the vital forces in the entire physiological system. It controls cell metabolism and growth, pulse rate and heat regulation. Its effect on the gonadals can also influence a person's sex. According to esoteric doctrine, the pituitary is the "inner light" of the cosmic consciousness or the "inner voice" of God (the inborn—not the acquired—conscience). In the dissociated ego-awareness of the incarnation the link with the Divine "primitive fire" or "cosmic tone" OM is interrupted. But we can reopen the "roof" of our skullcaps by meditation and thus achieve "illumination" or pure "vibration" of "Divine immediacy" (Master Ekkehart) (see the chapter on the supraconscious).

This energy centre vibrates most intensively when in its active state and also exercises its greatest influence on people while they are meditating. The sensitive sees colours like those of a magnificent rainbow firework display (the aura).

No. 2, The Energy Centre of Strength

The energy centre of strength lies in the loins and in the backbone near the adrenalin gland, between the hip-bone and the ribs. The adrenalin glands are the ones that go to work when there is anger, aggravation or agitation; in states such as these they augment their secretion of adrenalin, thus causing increased disharmony. The adrenalin glands are connected with the sympathetic nerve, a representative of the subconscious.

The sensitive sees the following colours: light-red to orange (in cases of anger, aggravation and agitation, red-brown to scarlet).

No. 3, The Energy Centre of Judgement

The energy centre of judgement lies in the solar plexus, in the hollow of the abdomen, near the pancreas; the pancreatic enzyme plays an important part in the metabolism of fats and protein. The pancreas also secretes the vital insulin so important in blood-sugar balance and the metabolism of carbohydrate. This centre is attributed to the subconscious and is called the seat of personal memory (the sun Chakra). For the sensitive it is the first level of ESP (extra-sensory perception). For this reason all sensitives would be well advised to protect this centre with silk day and night and particularly during meditation so that it may function without hindrance (silk keeps away evil influences). The sensitive sees the following colours: light-red and green.

No. 4, The Energy Centre of Love

The energy centre of love lies in the region of the heart on the breastbone, near the thymus gland. The centre of love is the source of divine light in the human body. It regulates the functions of the heart and the circulatory system and is subordinated to the subconscious.

For us healers it is also a spiritual centre since it is a particularly important factor in healing. Here we find the second level of clairvoyance, controlled psycho-kinetic power. The love of God is transmitted by the human heart. It effects intuitive comprehension of inter-human relations and all natural events. It is the "quiet voice" that speaks in your soul. The sensitive sees the following colours: variously glowing golden radiations right through to rose and deep purple.

No. 5, The Energy Centre of Power

The energy centre of power lies at the back of the throat in a brain centre situated at the root of the tongue near the thyroid gland which governs physical equilibrium, metabolism and the respiratory system. It takes effect below the medulla oblongata and in a forward direction towards the larynx (throat Chakra). It is the field of vibration of our positive and negative words (centre of speech) and determines how articulate we are. It is attributed to our subconscious. The sensitive sees the colours silvery-blue and blue-green.

No. 6, The Energy Centre of Imagination

The energy centre of imagination lies between the eyes, near the root of the eye and opposite the pineal gland. This centre is called the Third Eye and is the third level of extra-sensory perception. Its name is the "Jewel of Differentiation" or the "Eye of God", i.e. instruction, commandment, order, insight, vision. It is the seat of creativity and divine intelligence (inspiration). When this centre is activated you must be aware that, as of now, "the Gate of the Spirit" opens for you and your higher self becomes effective, since it is here that you receive the Holy Ghost (the Pneuma of the Greeks, the Atman of the Indians).

Here clear, logical thinking and healthy judgement are anchored; this is why the centre is attributed to the conscious. In the course of years of regular meditation you will feel healing flowing through your arms and hands right into the tips of your fingers, through the whole of the subtle body, to strengthen your personality. In teletherapy this energy centre is of pre-eminent importance. The sensitive will see the following colours: yellow, pink, lily white right through to deep blue or violet.

No. 7, The Energy Centre of Understanding

The energy centre of understanding lies above the eyes in the centre of the forehead. It is our centre of light and peace and is attributed to the conscious. If you develop your spiritual power of understanding, your whole organism will be grateful since, by your frankness and tolerance in understanding, you eliminate the physical and psychic obstructions that are one of the main causes of imperfect health. The sensitive will see the following colours: shades ranging from pink to lilac, light apple green.

No. 8, The Energy Centre of the Will

The energy centre of the will lies in the middle of the forehead in the forebrain, just above the centre of understanding. This is why they are called the twin centres and work hand in hand. They are attributed to the conscious. The will is the cornerstone of healing—"Lord, your will be done; into your hands I commend my spirit."

Through the willing of a return of health, that is of a "voluntary" desire to allow God's will to be wrought in you, you automatically ally yourself with the forces of intuitive understanding. That is why Master Ekkehart says, "When we know what we ought to do, then that happens which we want to."

The sensitive will see the following colours: lemon to primrose yellow, emerald green.

No. 9, the Energy Centre of Order

The energy centre of order lies beneath the solar plexus at the navel and is attributed to the subconscious (navel Chakra). If you are suffering from disturbances in the abdomen-stomach-intestine region, the reason lies in a disharmony of body, soul and spirit, i.e. there is too little order in the areas of feeling and life. However, you are perfectly capable of bringing order out of your inner disorder in that you consciously control and correct your spiritual "digestion" through your emotions and dreams (psychic hygiene). In this way you can cleanse your past and build up your future during the present time.

The sensitive will see the following colours: leaden grey in the case of disharmony, green in the case of harmony.

No. 10, The Energy Centre of Initiative

The energy centre of initiative (courage and enthusiasm) lies at the thickened commencement of the backbone at the basis of the brain, in the neck. Because of its activity it is called the fire centre and is attributed to the conscious. The activation of courage and enthusiasm generates a tremendously positive vibration throughout your entire nervous system which makes you capable of peak performance much as a wind-fanned fire rapidly spreads. The sensitive will see the following colours: fiery orange to red.

No. 11, The Energy Centre of Elimination

The energy centre of elimination lies at the lower end of the backbone in the sacrum and coccyx and is connected with the adrenalin glands. These glands control the chemical compositon of the body fluids, the urogenital system. This centre is attributed to the subconscious and is also concerned with the spiritual "elimination" of all that is negative, of relinquishing and renunciation, of forgiving and forgetting.

The sensitive will see the following colours: orange to red.

No. 12, The Energy Centre of Life

The energy centre of life lies in the genital organs and is connected with the left tract of the sympathetic nervous system. It controls the sexual functions and is called the root-bearer lotus or the root centre. This centre accommodates extremely powerful vital energy. From here, in the course of (healing) meditation, you can send your vibrations into the higher energy centres and thus awaken them. When you have activated this centre, which is profoundly linked with the subconscious, you will become aware of the most marked change, for when the spirit-saturated vital force ("Kundalini") reaches the crown centre, the sun of the organ of light can shine the brightest. In this way you will experience a tremendous strengthening of your vital physical forces, of psychic harmony and of spiritual awareness.

Spiritual Causes and Sources of our Sicknesses

A. In General

If you want to restore yourself to health, you can do this only through active co-operation, through a powerful determination to recover and implicit confidence that you can be perfectly healthy. Begin in a moment of quiet to think about the life you lead and ask yourself:

Why have I fallen ill?

What can I do about it?

Is it my constant fears, my primitive fears?
fear of life?
fear of losing my livelihood?
fear of growing old?
fear of loneliness?
fear concerning my partner?
fear of examinations?
fear of crowds?
fear of death?

I can consciously face up to my fear by carefully thinking through and, if possible, experiencing that which I fear. In this way I reduce my fears, build up courage and confidence in myself and am finally proud of the victory gained over myself.

Is it all the cares and problems I find to worry about every day, making life unnecessarily complicated?
Have I got myself into a vicious circle of negative thought?

I can practise thinking more positively day by day, developing more self-confidence and trust in God, confronting difficulties more actively.

Is it a lack of endurance? Am I too quickly discouraged? Do I too quickly give in to paralyzing resignation?

I can accept life and, in future, concentrate not on sickness, disability and defeat, but on health, advancement and up-swing. I set myself cheerful and constructive aims.

Do I feel misunderstood and dissatisfied?

I must reduce my ego by thinking more of those around me and of giving.

Do I expect too much of my partner, my children, the people around me? Is this why I am constantly being disappointed?

If I cease to expect anything of other people and start expecting everything of myself instead, I can no longer be disappointed. I realize that everyone is an independent personality and has exactly the same rights as I have. I therefore expect nothing of them at all but shall gladly allow them all to surprise me!

Am I full of hate, envy, rancour, anger, jealousy and dissatisfaction?

I must daily increase and develop my ability to love since a lack of love is the root of all evil.

Am I unable to forgive?

Although I have been hurt and my feelings injured, I must learn to forgive, otherwise I cannot recover good health. Only those that are completely free from negative thoughts and feelings can, in the long run, remain healthy.

Is it the stress of my studies, of work, in my private life that is ruining my health?

I shall not allow anyone, not even myself, to expect too much of me. I know that my health is more important than the most important "duty" since, if I am ill, I can fulfil no duties at all. I ensure that I get sufficient sleep and exercise to compensate, at least regular forest walks in the fresh air.

Is it environmental influences (constant exposure to stimuli, pollution, civilizational disease)?

I shall no longer allow myself to be negatively influenced by radio, press and television; I shall live in a way acceptable to myself and my environment.

Is my soul cut off from the spiritual worlds and the natural sources of life by fundamental disbelief?

Since, with no faith at all, human beings cannot live, I shall do everything in my power to find a sensible faith or to reconcile faith and knowledge.

Do I make my own life and that of others difficult by my bossiness and know-it-all attitude?

I practise humility, modesty, consideration and tolerance every day.

Do feelings of guilt and self-torture prevent me from living in a carefree manner?

I try to make good any injustice I have inflicted and to be more consistently righteous. I am a child of God who forgives even the worst sinners so that I have nothing to fear from Him if I allow myself to be guided by my conscience.

Is it faults in my upbringing, the fact that I received too little affection and attention or even that I was repressed or maltreated that bother me?

I cannot change what has happened. But spiritual hurts can heal just like physical ones if they be treated properly. I have grown up and have left childhood behind. I take control of my own life and work to improve myself. I give my own children and all those around me the loving understanding that I would have given so much for during my own childhood, and in this way I, too, shall become whole.

B. In Particular

The Addictions

Here again I must draw attention to the affluence of the Western World since the folk in the Third World have no money for the satisfaction of addictions; they are well content when they are able to buy the basic essentials of life. Affluence in conjunction with a lack of common sense is worse than privation. Addictions have the most various psychic causes—loneliness, stress, the struggle for power, pressure, fears, self-defence, disgust, depression, cowardice, weakness, inexperience, dissatisfaction, bedazzlement or infatuation, desperation, but also exuberance and over indulgence; in all cases it is a running away from life, from responsibility and from the acceptance of the full human state which, of course, includes the overcoming of all the difficulties involved.

1. Gluttony, Overweight

The glutton is always in search of love, encouragement and reward. He numbs his dissatisfied ego with sweets and literally devours everything that comes to hand. In this way he fills his emotional vacuum and quietens the unbearable sadness caused by what he—or she—sees as a lack of attention and affection. Physical repleteness is thus a replacement for the lacking psychic fulfilment. Later on the glutton gets even less affection since his gross appearance makes him unattractive. On top of all this he gets cross with himself because of his lack of self-control and thus he finds himself caught in a vicious circle of drastic dieting and uninhibited, greedy eating. These people are constantly expecting dissatisfaction. They forget to give others genuine affection and are then disappointed when they do not get the love they expect. These people can be helped if they set aside their egocentric thinking and adjust themselves permanently to giving instead of taking. Stand naked in front of a big mirror every day and for five minutes imagine yourself as weighing what you consider to be your ideal weight. This visualization will give you the strength to put your ideas into practice.

Get regular advice from a nutritional advisor for a long period of time and you will be surprised how pleasant good, wholesome food tastes. Go and meet people with the same problems as yours. There are diet clubs in almost every big town in many countries—Weight Watchers, for example, are very successful.

Exercise:

I am slender. I eat and drink only what my body requires. I give everyone I meet a happy smile. I radiate affection. I am satisfied. I am strong. I am a child of God.

Practise this exercise every day until you have reached your ideal weight.

2. Alcohol

In this case we are talking about the uninhibited drinker, whereby it is possible and, indeed, necessary to differentiate between this kind of drinker and the serious disease of alcoholism; this can be done on the basis of the characteristic symptoms. The drinker has the urge to hang on to "something liquid". He anaesthetizes his conflicts, fears and problems which he—or she—is not prepared to discuss with his—or her—partner. He feels himself suppressed and ruled over; so he numbs himself with alcohol, drinks to acquire Dutch courage, makes friends quickly with Tom, Dick and Harry but he remains stuck on the surface of things. Numbed as he is, he pulls the wool over his own eyes, imagining that all is well with the world, and he rapidly becomes a figure of ridicule. Instead of taking him seriously, people feel sorry for him and that makes him angry and then he gets violent.

The drinker needs an advisor, a psychologist or a psychiatrist, to whom he can confide his conflicts, fears and problems. He must be prepared to let someone help him. If he does not do this he will have to be prepared for his wife and children to leave him, since the negative atmosphere he creates, which wears people out and breaks them up, and causes spiritual privation, suffering and misery, is an imposition on all his relations. If you are prepared to go to work on yourself, practise this exercise every day until you have been "dried out".

Exercise:

I do not like alcohol. I couldn't care less about the bottle. Nor about the glass. I feel a rebirth of responsibility in myself. I accept life as it is. I am strong. I am ready to discuss my problems.

3. Nicotine

The smoker has many unfulfilled yearnings. There is the desire for love and security, for freedom, communication and recognition. He fills a certain emptiness in his life by smoking because he has, oh, so many wishes. Then there is the fear of being caught red-handed. The cigarette, cigar or pipe became a substitute like the baby's dummy—one can "hang on" to it so well and hide one's nervousness. Full of apparent satisfaction, the smoker throws up what amounts to a smokescreen to hide the real objective, thus signalling clearly that he is unable to cope with his problems (dissatisfied women, unsuccessful men).

Smoking is worse than drinking:
1. One can smoke at one time a lot more than one can drink (chain smokers) since one's ability to function properly is not so immediately apparent (intoxication).
2. In return, serious damage results because, while alcohol is broken down and eliminated by the body, nicotine is only slightly and tar not at all.
3. The drinker does not disturb the people around him so long as he is not drunk but the smoker forces everyone in his vicinity to become "passive smokers".
4. Since many vegetarians and esoterics avoid alcohol but cannot escape from the grips of nicotine, the danger of addiction appears here to be particularly great. Hence a gradual cutting down is generally unsuccessful; a radical effort of will is required to cease smoking overnight.

Exercise:
I see my goal clearly before me. In the course of the years I shall do everything in my power to master my difficulties and to turn my wishes into reality. Cigarettes are of no importance to me. They taste dreadful. I am determined to reach my goal and overcome my problems.

4. Drugs

The problem of drugs is similar to that of drinking since it is also an effort to escape from anxiety, cares and conflicts. In the course of the years my attention has been drawn in particular to drug addiction in intellectuals whose complaint is always the same—"more and more is constantly being expected of me . . ." Is it really or do they merely imagine that this is so? They are under personal and professional pressure and a tranquillizer rapidly makes way for hard drugs which gradually lead to disintegration of the personality. When success, performance, power and recognition fail to quench the overpowering thirst for love, the next step is escape into the world of illusion. Slow but sure self-destruction overcomes the drug addict. I have found that, if these people ever decide to get well again, the only thing that helped them was the power of love and faith. I should like to recount a crass example I met in the course of my healing activities. On the advice of his parents—whom I had known for years—a student addicted to heroin came to me. His parents stood by him and did all they were able to understand his perilous situation. He was in a terrible state; I found him revolting but I recalled a letter my father had written me citing the words of Jesus, "Whatever you shall do for the least of these my brothers, you will have done for me." I concentrated on the young man's problem and told him that its roots lay in a struggle for ascendancy between himself and his girl-friend who was also studying and whose progress was much faster than his own, a circumstance he freely admitted. I explained that he would have to find a way out of this situation himself, inasmuch as his love was strong enough and he was prepared to do an about face in his thinking and become aware of his own true value. I treated him—unwillingly because he smelled abominably—and gave him to understand that, if he wanted to come again, I should expect him to appear washed and combed and generally looking presentable. A week later he came back—all spick and span and well dressed; I could hardly believe my eyes. He told me that he was going on holiday with his girl-friend to Greece where they planned to discuss the whole situation. I was impressed. On his return he came a last time, brown and full of self-confidence and the joy of living. Thanks to the sensitivity of his girl-friend, who loved him and had faith in him and was tactful enough to make him feel more of a man by understating her own academic progress, he was cured for good.

Exercise:

Drugs are immaterial to me. I shall no longer seek consolation in them. I am positive. I am successful. I am satisfied with my achievements. I am content with God, the world and myself.

A Special Word to Young People

The five senses of today's young people are totally saturated—over-stimulated visually and aurally by the rapidly changing lights and the loud music of the discos, by neon signs, the cinema, television, background music even when they are studying, traffic noise etc. As a result of this overtaxing of the senses, young people yearn for extra-sensory experience. They take drugs, they numb themselves and the sixth sense goes into action in the form of illusions. Then there is the rude awakening which is not the case when the sixth sense operates properly. Man is a child of God and religious by nature. Thus young people, whose senses are saturated, constantly desire subconsciously to return to God and find peace in him. But they can do this only by seeking quiet and allowing all their senses to calm down; then, through meditation, they will once again find God and the true sixth sense. It is only thus that they will regain their inner balance and achieve harmony with their environment.

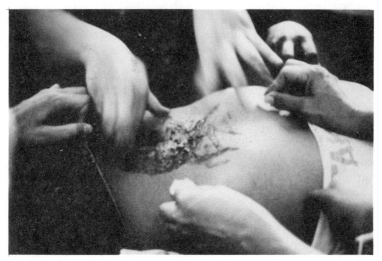

Josephine Sison operating in 1981; her fingers move quick as lightning while she is in trance.

Various Diseases and Conditions with Exercises to Activate the Appropriate Energy Centre

To enable you more quickly to recognize your health problems and their true cause, to prevent your becoming bogged down in a mire of self-pity and, should you be at home or away, to allow you immediately to commence the necessary spiritual exercises, I am giving below a list of what my experience has shown to be the most common illnesses and stressful situations. First of all, you must be aware that sickness is basically no more than the manifestation of our own errors, passions and addictions, dissatisfactions and lack of rectitude, of our wrong-thinking and doing—in short, of our failure to respect the Ten Commandments.

It must become a matter of pre-eminent importance that you admit your weaknesses, mistakes and the error of your ways generally *to yourself*, that you forgive yourself and strive at a spiritual level to better yourself. In this way you will in future be able to make for yourself a healthy life worth living. It is truly well worthwhile.

You can do the following spiritual exercise every day. As described in the section on healing meditation, go and sit in a quiet corner (your legs must never be crossed if you are sitting on a chair), lay your hands in your lap, palms upward, relax, breathe deeply in and out three times and read this exercise through three times, preferably out loud so that you feel the effect of your words; then close your eyes and let what you have read echo for a while in your mind. Soon you will begin to feel eased. You will be better able to master your difficulties and obtain an overview of the situation. By virtue of this renewal of the vital forces within you, by your satisfaction and positive attitude, you will be successful in both your private and professional life, since through you divine love, divine life, divine truth and wisdom are now working.

But before continuing to the exercise I must explain what *the right and the left sides of the body* are in the context of the secret doctrine. The right side is masculine (male) and symbolizes the external, professional and social life; wisdom, intelligence and truth. A man fights with his right hand and gives his wife the necessary protection therewith. The right side is the portal of giving.

If you have pain on this side of your body, ask yourself seriously which man in your private, professional or social life has upset you. Whom must you forgive to permit the pain to diminish?

Have you misused your thinking and offended against wisdom and honesty? Have you practised too much financial, intellectual or emotional reserve, thus setting up obstacles within yourself? Should you not be prepared to give more, to open yourself up more?

Exercise:

Divine intelligence is flowing through me. I radiate the strength of divine wisdom. By virtue of God's spirit I am able to master all the problems life brings. I am shown the path I am to take. Divine intelligence guides and leads me to perfect achievement. I am the personification of divine wisdom.

The left side is feminine (female) and symbolizes the inner life, that of the emotions and the family. The woman holds her husband with her left arm, the one nearest the heart. Feminine means life and love. The left side is the portal of acceptance and devotion.

If you frequently suffer from pains on the left side, ask yourself: Which female person has angered me in the past and why have I tried to bury this matter? Whom must I forgive so that I may be relieved of my pain? Have I abused the spiritual power of love? Have I permitted a relationship that brings unhappiness, or have I myself been misused, deceived and exploited? In my pride, have I refused the good that was offered me? Were there people I could have helped with my spiritual resources? Why have I refrained from so doing up till now?

Exercise:

Divine good pulses through my life. I am the recipient of divine love. I receive good and transmit it to others. The all-loving, all-giving power of God shall henceforth release me from all resentment and bitterness of past and present. I am divine understanding. I am divine life, divine purity and love.

Menopause:

To enable men and women better to cope with the "change of life" it requires in the first line a positive attitude to life and to Nature. Mettlesome, vivacious women suffer far more from hot flushes during this time than their less passionate sisters. But they should accept this as a sign of Nature. The regular consumption of sage decoction and a foregoing of coffee and alcohol will ease these hot flushes.

When your children have grown up you should seek a fulfilling occupation so that your personality can flourish anew and radiate the joy of living. By virtue of the security innate in motherliness and fatherliness, mature men and women are able to show so much love and deep understanding for so many everyday things. Always try to transmit your accumulated wisdom to the young people around you. Be constantly receptive for new ideas and take a course now and again in a subject that interests you so that your life is given fresh impetus and a new source of fulfilment for a long time to come. And never forget that all the changes life undergoes come at precisely the right moment.

Exercise:

Activate the spiritual powers of energy centres No. 12, life; No. 4, love; No. 7, understanding.

The acceptance of life strengthens my spirit, my soul and my body. I am filled with divine life. Divine love flows through my muscles, my organs, nerves, glands and cells. My eyes shine, my skin is beautifully soft and smooth. There is a gentle smile on my lips, full of divine understanding and giving. I pass without difficulty through every change life brings and am in harmony with Nature. Divine joy, love and gratitude are the sources of my positive attitude.

Examinations:

Is my fear of the coming examinations merely subjecting me to more pressure and what can I do about it?

Exercise:

Mobilize the spiritual powers of energy centre No. 1, faith.

I am completely calm and relaxed. Divine intelligence will tell me the right answer at the right time. By virtue of divine intelligence I am capable of achieving success. I am full of divine intelligence—I *am* divine intelligence. I am completely calm and relaxed. Divine intelligence is working in me most wonderfully.

Nerves:

When you are tortured by serious problems and cares and you feel that your partner, your children, your studies, your business or your job are demanding too much of you, when there are too many things that make you so irritable and overwrought thay you make life hell for yourself and all those around you, ask yourself in a quiet moment: What exactly is getting on my nerves? Why am I so irritable, dissatisfied, impatient, restless? Is it that I want to dominate others? Why can I no longer put up with the people around me? What is the true reason for my spleen and who is it that arouses my aggressiveness? Where exactly should I start "tidying up"?

Exercise:

Mobilize energy centres No. 4, love; No. 6, imagination; No. 9, order; No. 12, life.

Divine order is flowing through my nervous system. Order and satisfaction fills me. I am completely calm and relaxed. From now on I shall dominate and judge no one. Divine order is within me. Within me is divine peace. I am tranquil and relaxed. I am divine love. Divine love supports me. Divine love lightens my heart. Divine love fills me with harmony and solves all my problems. Divine love fills my consciousness with happy, helpful thoughts. Divine love is flowing through me and warming me, giving me a feeling of deep security. Divine gratitude accompanies my words. My nervous system is imbued with divine life and peace.

Bladder:

The spiritual cause of problems with the urinary bladder is reluctance to let go of sons and daughters, of people once loved, of experiences which belong to the past and are basically no more than unnecessary ballast.

Ask yourself: What are the people and the things from which I must now free myself? Whose influence must I lay aside in order to live more independently in the present? Am I full of erroneous judgements, bitterness, impatience, vengeful thoughts, feelings of injustice?

Exercise:

Mobilize energy centres No. 9, order; No. 11, elimination.

I now free myself from all negative thoughts and misconceptions. I am filled with divine order. I willingly let go of . . . (my daughter, my son, a once-loved person, past experiences, etc.). I am released from my fears, my bitterness, my secret thoughts of revenge, my impatience, my feelings of injustice and misunderstanding which enthral my body in disorder and block my bladder. Divine order flows through my body. Divine order cleanses my spirit of all ambiguous situations and eliminates them from my body. All that burdened me has been eliminated. I am divine order.

Bed-wetting:

The true reason for bed-wetting is a deep spiritual weeping. You are unable at the moment to communicate your feelings to someone who is of importance to you or you feel that the person in question does not understand you. Your subconsciousness weeps at night because you cannot yet cope with the harsh world and yearn for protection and security, for love and confidence, tenderness and warmth, so that your sensitive soul need no longer weep.

For children: What is it that makes me cry? I want my father and mother and my brothers and sisters to understand and love me better and not to quarrel all the time. I should like to get stronger. Please help me. I also have trouble at school, with my teacher and the other children. Please help me.

For parents: What makes my child cry? How can I help my child better to cope with the world? Are there too many quarrels and tensions in our family? Do I give my child sufficient genuine affection, warmth, time and security? Do I protect him/her sufficiently from the negative influence of television? Does my child go to sleep calmly?

A word to all parents: *Never forget that children are thoughts of the spirit and the representatives of life, truth and love.*

Exercise:

(To be done preferably by children and parents together.)

Mobilize the spiritual powers No. 4, love; No. 9, order; No. 12, life; No. 2, strength; No. 10, courage.

God's love flows through me and solves all my problems before I go to sleep. I go to sleep in God's peace. I can talk to mummy and daddy about my problems and they will understand me. I can talk to my teacher about my fears and he/she will understand me. I can talk to the other children at school and ask them to help me. I am not alone with my problems. God's love surrounds me. I am carried along in the warmth of God's arms. My guardian angel watches over me day and night. I am full of God's strength and God's courage. I am full of God's love and harmony. I am strong. I am strong! I am God's strength!

Heart and Blood Vessels:

The spiritual causes of diseases which attack the heart and the blood vessels lie in the disrupted, hypersensitive, frozen and unexpressed affections. That is to say that the sufferer yearns for love and fulfilment and hungers for recognition but, because of unfortunate experiences with certain people that he has not been able to put behind him, he is incapable himself of showing affection. *Angina pectoris* is a sign of the contraction, the cold-heartedness and the wilfulness which result from the sufferer's own stubborn behaviour. You feel hurt and downtrodden, unjustly treated by those close to you who have left you behind in your bitterness. You feel dreadfully offended and forgiveness is a thing that is oh, so difficult for you to grapple with!

Immoderate smoking and drinking, greasy food and too much coffee promote this obstruction of the blood vessels and the consequences are high blood pressure, all kinds of cramp, a gangrenous condition of the legs due to excessive smoking, arteriosclerosis, cardiac infarction, embolism and thrombosis. Destructive thoughts of wilfully not wanting to repent, hate, envy, rancour, jealousy and egoism stop up the blood vessels and thus block the flow of life itself—for it must never be forgotten that your life flows through your blood vessels.

Jesus said to the desciples, "Do you still not see or understand? Are your hearts hardened?" (*Mark* 8:17).

Since the heart is the only organ that is immune to attack by cancer—because it is the seat of love and all the other emotions and can at all times be activated and its circulation improved by a change in your thinking—you should ask yourself in a moment of quiet whether your heart is not constricted by cold-heartedness and wilfulness; whether your head does not rule your heart; what events in your life (be they in regard to the heart or your professional life) are literally blocking your veins and arteries. Ask yourself where you can direct your thoughts to avoid the palpitations that distress you. In cases of heart cramp ask yourself in what secret and insurmountable matter of the heart you are unbending, ask where you should tidy up your life and where you could demonstrate your feelings more freely. Where should you be more courageous? Where should you think more of loving and giving instead of always concentrating on taking? Whom are you repulsing? Whom must you forgive?

It is well worthwhile thinking about these matters of the heart since the open-hearted giving and receiving of love is the greatest remedy in the world.

Exercise:

Mobilize the spiritual powers No. 4, love; No. 7, understanding; No. 8, will-power and No. 12, life.

Divine love frees me from all bitterness and destructive thoughts with regard to my neighbour. Divine love encompasses my heart. Divine understanding warms and increases the flow of blood to my heart. In me is reflected perfect love and I radiate joy and vitality. Those around me love me with the love of Christ. Divine love flows through my heart and my blood vessels and gives fresh impetus to my life. Divine love makes me free and happy. Divine love implies giving and understanding. I am the expression of divine love which is, by nature, perfect. Let not my will but your will be done, O Lord.

Headache and Migraine:

The spiritual causes of headache and migraine are conflicts between one's appetites and one's thinking, an occlusion or blockage of one's activities, particularly at a sexual level which is also known to us as the "spiritual orgasm".

Since the throat is the zone of equilibrium between head and heart, that is to say between two partners (be they man and woman, daughter or son, boss or business partner or colleague etc.), and you have tried in vain to impose your will upon this partner, it often happens that a headache develops in the regions behind the throat or that the neck becomes stiff, blocking the blood supply to the head. This abuse of one's spiritual forces paralyses one's activities. It means that you are disappointed, you brood too much because you have expected too much from your partner or someone else near to you and the aggression that thus develops can manifest itself as a headache. You retreat into bed, draw the curtains and shut yourself up in your room. You cannot bear even the slightest noise and your only wish is to be left alone—that is, you run away from yourself.

Because of this embodied aggression you can and will not give yourself sexually to your partner and the occlusion of these activities causes you to relegate your appetites to your head and the result is this "spiritual orgasm".

Find a quiet moment and ask yourself honestly why you brood too much, thus literally "cracking your head". Are you ambitious or obstinate? Do you ask too much of your partner (or those around you) at a professional or a private level? Why do you avoid facing up to your sexual problems? And why don't you try dealing with their causes? Are you honestly prepared to do something about this? Then do get on with it—it is so well worthwhile. Be active!

Exercise:

Mobilize the spiritual powers No. 2, strength; No. 4, love; No. 1, faith; No. 7, understanding; No. 9, order; No. 12, life.

Borne on the wings of divine understanding, divine order develops in my life and flows through the blood vessels of my brain. My mind, my body and my soul are filled with divine, rejuvenating life. Divine understanding and order solve all my problems. My life is filled with faith and strength. Divine love fills my heart and gives me thoughts of divine understanding. I am filled with divine strength and open-hearted love; I am encompassed by joyous life. I am the expression of perfect love.

Eyes:

Seeing means understanding. The eyes signify spiritual recognition—not material, but mental. With outward vision in mind, Jesus said, "Do you have eyes but fail to see?" (*Mark* 8:18).

Thus the spiritual cause of eye disease is the unwillingness to "see the light", to let things in. Your eyes are there to give you insight into everything. If this gift is abused, the nerves and muscles become cramped and this causes a reduction in the blood supply so that you over-strain your eyes.

If you are prepared to go to work on yourself, I suggest that you take off your spectacles or contact lenses as often as possible, go walking in the open air, strengthen your eyes by looking at the green of the fields and the gay colours and regularly do eye exercises. You will then very soon recognize what you really cannot see and what you do not want to see. Don't resign yourself to having bad eyesight, but do something about it. Find activities in the open air so that your circulation is promoted—your eyes will be grateful. And ask yourself in a moment of quiet: are there things in my life that I prefer not to see or that I do not wish to have brought home to me? Am I afraid of seeing things as they really are? Where do I set up obstacles between myself and self-recognition? Do I pay enough attention to world affairs? Have I abused the spiritual power of initiative and deprived myself of valuable energies? Is this the reason why my eyes feel burnt, weak and unfocussed?

Exercise:

Mobilize the spiritual powers No. 6, imagination; No. 7, understanding; No. 8, will-power; No. 1, faith.

My eyes recognize the white, pure light of Chirst and are surrounded by the rays of its strength. They banish all darkness from my consciousness, my body and my soul. Pure, spiritual light and divine understanding are growing in me. I am filled with divine peace. I relax and let go. I take the time to give my eyes sufficient rest. I am filled with divine time . . . divine time . . . divine time. I am completely calm . . . completely calm . . . God's will flows through my eyes and becomes reality. I am divine light. I am perfect, divine light.

Ears:

Jesus said to the disciples, "(Do you have) ears but fail to hear?" (*Mark* 8:18)

The spirtual causes of ear disease lie in disobedence, egocentrism and constraint.

You prefer not to hear anything anyone says to you. That is to say, you are not sufficiently humble and ready to listen but prefer to go your egocentric way until the time comes when you are incapable of hearing anything at all. Then you will no longer hear whispering, the outward expression of your inability to experience anything at all. This sudden deafness requires you without notice to listen inwardly and warns you against further disobedience. So listen within you and ask yourself in a moment of quiet what it is that you do not want to hear from others. Whom do you refuse to obey? Why are you so egocentric? Must you become more humble? Have you misused the power of faith?

Exercise:
Mobilize the spiritual powers No. 1, faith; No. 4, love; No. 7, understanding.
Faith fills my life. I have faith in humanity. Divine understanding flows through my spirit and my ears. I feel how mightily it works in me! Divine love encompasses my ears. Divine understanding fills my mind. I am faith, divine love and divine understanding.

Stomach—Intestines—Constipation—Diarrhoea—Heamorrhoids:

The spiritual causes of the various gastric and intestinal diseases are inner conflict, false judgement, aggression, repressed yearnings, hate, fear, injustice, feelings of bitterness, self-condemnation.
Chronic constipation means: you refuse to live in the present and you "constipate" your life with the garbage of your past. You take enough laxatives, heaven knows, to expel via your intestines as quickly as possible your fear of living in the present and coming to grips with it. Tidy up your life! Live in the present! It is worthwhile.
Drink a glass of lukewarm water every morning. Before going to bed rub your tummy clockwise with a herbal massage oil. Talk gently to your intestines and tell them that from now on you expect regular activity from them. Do everything you can to ensure your spiritual equilibrium—through balanced nutrition, physical activity and particularly by tidying up your thoughts.
Diarrhoea symbolizes your fear—you literally "fill your pants" from terror. This often happens to people facing examinations or some other event of prime importance.
Diarrhoea is the result of fear of failure.
Haemorrhoids symbolize sluggishness of thought or excessive anxiousness or irritability, for example in new situations or in regard to the future.

Find a quiet moment and ask yourself earnestly: What am I bottling up inside me, making life difficult for myself all day and every day? Why am I constantly digging around in the ruins of the past, all the while forgetting the present? What is it that I dream about so much that I block all other activity? Who is it that I condemn in such a way that my aggression merely increases? Whom must I forgive? Must I become more courageous so that my "secret" fears and terrors can be coaxed into more normal channels? With whom am I discontented? What are the reasons for these feelings of bitterness? And for my self-condemnation?

Once these questions are answered, set about clearing things up!

Exercise:

Mobilize spiritual powers No. 3, judgement; No. 4, love; No. 7, understanding; No. 9, order; No. 12, life.

I am filled with divine order. All negative thoughts of bitterness, injustice, fear, hate and self-punishment are banished from my soul. I am at divine peace with everyone. I have ceased all criticism and allow everybody to be successful, happy and content. I am divine equilibrium, divine life, divine love. My spirit is filled with divine purity which stands guard over my thoughts and deeds. I am filled with divine understanding and order. I am filled with profound gratitude.

Back:

In my experience there are many and varied reasons for back trouble—a build-up of irritation in the subconsciousness, pressures, intrigues and a struggle to get the upper hand in marriage, business or in one's social life, a lack of frankness, distrust, stubbornness, abuses in money matters and the fear of discovery, financial problems and living beyond one's means. False and dictatorial expressions of self-will leave their mark in the lower back.

The shoulders symbolize responsibility. Pain in the shoulders means that you must often carry a heavy "rucksack" full of problems around with you or that, just now, you have to carry a responsibility that is too much for you.

Ask yourself when you can find a quiet moment: Must I become honest and upright? Must I become stronger so that I may better cope with pressure and carry responsibility? Who is intriguing against me? Where must I be forgiving and send out thoughts of love? Do I allow my partner to dominate me?

Exercise:
Mobilize spiritual powers No. 2, strength; No. 1, faith; No. 4, love; No. 9, order; No. 10, initiative.
I am divine strength. Divine strength imbues my back and my shoulders. All anxiety leaves my body. I am capable of carrying responsibility. I am full of initiative! Divine courage and enthusiasm make me as strong as an oak. I am capable of coping with all the situations life brings since I am filled with divine order and love. I am filled with divine faith that helps me to solve all my future problems. The love, wisdom and divine strength of the spirit is working in me and making me a tower of strength!

Kidneys:

The spiritual causes of kidney disease lie in partnership problems, in chronic criticizing and in a deep desire for freedom and independence. Dialysis is often the last port in a storm but this becomes a "synthetic" partner and the desire for freedom and independence remains.

If you really want to solve your problem then you must be completely honest with yourself and your partner and discuss the matter until, between you, you have found a positive solution.

And may your desire for freedom and independence be never so strong, do not be tempted to tip the baby out with the bath—slowly does it, step by step, so that the next thing to disrupt your kidney function is not your overweening ambition. Pursue self-fulfilment by all means but keep a sense of proportion or else you might risk being carried away by your very happiness!

Sit down quietly and ask yourself: Do I have partnership problems and for how long have these existed? Have I caused them myself and why have I become bogged down in them? Are my fears the cause? Must I develop courage and honesty in order to find the ideal solution? What can I do to find myself and to relieve the congestion in my kidneys?

In the case of kidney stones: Where do I want to throw my kidney stones?

Exercise:

Mobilize spiritual powers No. 11, elimination; No. 9, order; No. 7, understanding.

I willingly let go of all negative thoughts and things. Elimination in me is unhindered and complete. I cleanse myself of a relationship that is a burden to me. From now on I am filled with divine order. I am filled with divine understanding in every situation with which life confronts me. Divine love gives me the strength to fulfil myself. I am divine order and I do not exaggerate. I love divine freedom and am worthy to step out along this path in gratitude and under the protection of divine love.

Lungs and Chest:

The spiritual causes of lung and chest disease lie in conflict, problems of the heart, disappointments, bitterness, resentment, hate, brooding, hurt, a lack of open-heartedness and feelings of aversion. The outward cause lies in smoking and the inhalation of exessive quantities of dust.

Cancer of the breast is often caused by opposition to somebody, by a serious shock such as the loss of a loved one through a fatal accident or the renunciation of an illicit love, by heartache and profound resignation.

Find a quiet corner and ask yourself: Is it not perhaps my own fault that I am always being disappointed? Do I ask too much? Why am I full of negative feelings like hate, resentment and bitterness? Why am I destroying myself with these thoughts and those around me by my negative thinking? Is it not high time that I forgave myself and those around me? Should I not slowly be thinking more of sending out thoughts of love and understanding? Why am I destroying myself by so much smoking?

Exercise:

Mobilize spiritual powers No.. 4, love; No. 7, understanding; No. 8, will-power; No. 9, order; No. 12, life.

Divine order and love for those around me is growing in me. Bitterness, rancour, hate and resentment leave my mind. I am capable of forgiving and from now on I allow everyone to be happy. I am divine understanding. The divine will guides me in all matters and contributes to resolving completely all conflicts. I liberate myself from excessive smoking, which merely serves me as a replacement for love, and I shall henceforth live on divine love which helps to carry me along and which strengthens my mind, my spirit and my body so that they may become the expression of perfection, joy and peace.

Fever and Infection:

The spiritual causes here always lie in disruptions of the emotions, that is, in conflicts that have taken on material form. By honesty and courage towards yourself and those around you, by the regular practise of sport, visits to the sauna, plenty of fresh air, a diet rich in vitamins and abstemiousness in regard to smoking and drinking, you will very soon become more resistant.

Ask yourself in a moment of quiet: Why are my emotions upset just now? What conflicts are a burden to me and am I just going to "chicken out"? What is it that I prefer not to see or admit to myself? Must I develop more courage? How can I become more resistant in future?

Exercise:

Mobilize spiritual powers No. 1, faith; No. 4, love; No. 7, understanding; No. 10, initiative.

I believe in myself and in the complete solution of my problem. I am full of a deep faith and this faith gives me tolerance and initiative at the right moment so that I can do the things that I have to do. I am full of courage and enthusiasm! Borne along by divine understanding and love and filled with deep faith, I am perfectly capable of coping with my life in future and of overcoming every emotional conflict with divine courage.

Asthma:

The spiritual reasons lie in difficulties of communication. As an asthma sufferer you yearn most desperately for affection. Because you want affection your breathing in is intensified but your breathing out is hindered because you find it difficult to give love to others. If you want to recover you must take a good look at all your fears, admit them honestly to yourself and set to work mercilessly upon yourself!

In a quiet moment ask yourself: Why do I feel so closed in? Of what and of whom am I afraid? Why am I always getting into conflict with people? Am I too intolerant? Who am I trying to manipulate through my attacks of asthma? Where and to whom can I show more affection?

Never forget that giving affection in the right place at the right time to those nearest to you will relieve you of the feeling of pressure so that you will be able to breathe more freely. Giving affords pleasure, understanding brings light, unity makes you strong.

Exercise:

Mobilize the spiritual powers No. 1, faith; No. 2, strength; No. 4, love; No. 5, power; No. 6, imagination; No. 7, understanding and No. 9, order.

I once more have faith in myself and those around me. Faith, faith, faith—this strong faith upholds me in divine understanding of my fellow men and gives me strength to manifest devoted divine love. The idea of divine love makes breathing in and out easier and frees me from all the fears that slumber secretly within me. Divine power flows through my spirit, my soul and my body and makes my breathing easier. I breathe freely, liberated by the love of Christ. I inhale in the love of Christ. I exhale in the love of Christ. I am the expression of divine love. I go in and out in divine understanding, in and out, in and out. I am the perfect expression of divine order.

Allergies:

The spiritual cause of allergies lies in substantialized aggression and is therefore frequently a continuation of asthma or skin diseases.

Ask yourself when you are quietly alone: Why do I repress the aggressiveness that is thus reflected in my body? Am I afraid of my sexuality or of becoming unclean in some way? Where do I want to be the centre of attraction? Am I prepared to give and receive more love?

You may do the exercises given in the case of asthma.

Skin Disorders:

The spiritual causes and sources of skin disorders lie in the (secret) passions, in the inner fire that cannot burn unrestricted, in the smouldering embers of your blood and in repressed anger. Something irritates you first internally and then externally. When you scratch you are symbolically digging to bury whatever you find unpleasant.

It is worthwhile finding a quiet moment in which to ask yourself: where can I further my sociability without inhibition? Is it really my aggressiveness towards those I feel do not understand me that irritates me? Has someone rejected me and do I find it difficult to forgive them because I do not understand? Is it my secret passions that I am always repressing. Why have I banished myself to isolation? Why do I torture myself? Is this caused by feelings of guilt and errors?

Exercise:

Mobilize the spiritual powers No. 4, love; No. 7, understanding; No. 8, will-power; No. 9, order.

I am completely calm and relaxed. All my fears and aggressiveness dissolve into nothing. Divine order is in me and this forgives everyone who has rejected me. Divine understanding liberates me from the prison of isolation and gives my soul divine love which I am capable of passing on to others. God's will be done in all my undertakings and make all I do successful. Divine order and divine understanding are in me. Divine love carries me throughout my life.

Inflamation of the Gall-bladder and Gallstones:

The spiritual cause of inflamation of the gall-bladder and gallstones is the pent-up exasperation one causes oneself. The petrification is the manifestation of an inner hardening resulting from resentment and hate. The operation for removal of the gallbladder forces you to think about yourself and your enemies, to forgive yourself and them, to stand back and take a good look at your exasperation and to begin anew in peace.

Ask yourself in a quiet moment: Who causes my bile to rise, who exasperates and "petrifies" me, who needs my forgiveness and about whom must I moderate my judgement? To whom must I send forgiveness and thoughts of love and understanding?

Exercise:

Mobilize the spiritual powers No. 4, love; No. 7, understanding; No. 9, order.

Divine love gives me the strength to forgive all those who weigh upon me. Resentment, hate and inner hardening leave me. I fill my heart with loving understanding. I no longer condemn anyone and I feel how divine order flows into my spirit, my soul and my body, making me joyous, free and happy. Divine love shall carry me all my life long.

Liver:

The spiritual causes of liver disease lie in constant feelings of guilt and self-condemnation, in injustices and unforgivingness, as well as in doubts about one's religious faith, in alcohol addiction and the immoderate consumption of such things as coffee, chocolate and nicotine.

Sit down and ask yourself: For what must I forgive myself in order to put the past behind me? How are things with my faith? Where is the happy medium? Do I feel bitter and resentful against someone who has treated me unfairly? Do I need to forgive them? Am I far to critical? Am I over-anxious?

Exercise:

Mobilize the spiritual powers No. 1, faith; No. 7, understanding; No. 8, will-power; No. 9, order and No. 12, life.

Christ guides me throughout my whole life and strengthens me in my faith. I believe in all those things that have the effect for me of the happy medium and bring the perfect solution for all my affairs. God's wisdom and truth lead me to loving understanding and forgiveness. I am willing to lay all my cares and burdens in the lap of divine order which will lend me perfect life. I am divine life, divine love, divine truth. I am divine light.

Throat:

The spiritual causes of throat diseases lie in obstinacy, in negative words or thoughts, in putting up with and "swallowing" things. Obstinacy causes swollen tonsils, sinus pain, inflamation of the throat, irritation of the nose, colds and even tonsilitis. Negative words cause a rough throat; complaining, reproachful words cause goitre and excresence; irritating words cause a nervous cough. Since the spiritual centre of power and strength manifests itself in the vocal chords, the tongue, the tonsils and the larynx, it is worthwhile to pay more attention to the spoken word and to formulate what you say lovingly.

Ask yourself in a quiet moment: Why do I condemn those around me? Why am I always criticizing my partner, the children, the neighbours, friends and acquaintances? Why am I dissatisfied deep down inside me? Why am I so easily offended? What can I do to keep myself under better control?

Exercise:

Mobilize the spiritual forces No. 1, faith; No. 3, judgement; No. 5, power; No. 6, imagination; and No. 7, understanding.

Divine strength is working powerfully through my body, soul and spirit, affecting all my affairs and liberating me from all negative influence. Divine order cleanses all my thoughts, words and actions and affords me loving, godly understanding of all those I meet. The divine grace of my faith renews the cells of my body and grants me success in all my undertakings all my life long. I am divine gratitude, divine love, divine truth and divine life.

Diabetes:

The spiritual cause of diabetes lies in constant exasperation and daily agitation, in harsh condemnation of oneself and others. All these burdens make it difficult for the pancreas to function properly and this means that the body is no longer able to metabolize sugar. If you wish to return to health you must subject yourself to a long period of spiritual cleansing.

Ask yourself in a moment of quiet: Why do I keep on getting unnecessarily worked up? Why do my partner and other people get on my nerves? Do I expect too much? Do I want to dominate others? Why am I so touchy regarding certain remarks? Why do I condemn myself, thus making my life difficult? Why do I condemn others?

Exercise:

Mobilize the spiritual powers No. 9, order; No. 3, judgement; No. 7, understanding; No. 2, strength; No. 1, faith.

I leave judgement to the divine law of justice. Divine peace enfolds my body, soul and spirit. I criticize and condemn no one and I, too, am no longer criticized, condemned or unjustly treated. Divine peace, grace and goodness are in me and I radiate these gifts to all those about me. Divine order shall in future govern all my affairs and relations. Divine strength affords me the certainty that I shall understand everyone in future and leave them to be and act as they see fit. I set aside my pride, resentment and envy, ceding them to divine order. I accuse neither myself nor others of any fault whatever. My egoism has left me. The power of divine understanding allows me to live in perfect harmony with my partner, my children and all others around me. I am filled with faith, divine strength and love. I am a perfect child of God.

Rheumatism, Arthritis, Arthrosis:

The spiritual causes of these diseases are:
Rheumatism: secret fears, constant criticism and nagging of those around you. This cramps the muscles and inflammation of the joints results. Finally, the bones dry out.

Thoughts of bitterness, disappointment and condemnation destroy the cells of the body, harden the blood vessels and block the flow of vital forces throughout your entire system.

Arthritis: contradictory feelings and unsolved problems.
Arthrosis: rigidity of thought, action and reaction towards others—our joints symbolize mutual relations. A dessicated way of thinking is inconducive to life and tends to dry out the bones. If you want to return to a life free from pain you must free yourself from your authoritarian ways, cultivate more sensitivity for the feelings of others and think a great deal more about giving. That is to say, you must cease sunning yourself in self-pity and go to work on yourself energetically. You should also ensure that you get plenty of fresh air and sunshine and that you are surrounded by harmony and warmth. If you transmit this warmth to those around you in the form of loving thoughts and feelings, it will immediately reflect back upon you positively.

So ask yourself in a quiet moment: Why do I always criticize and nag those around me? Where do my secret fears lie? Why am I so embittered? How can I resolve my conflicts? Should I not free myself from my authoritarian ways and acquire more humility? Should I become more sensitive to the feelings of those around me? Should I try to increase my physical and spiritual activity?

Exercise:

Mobilize the spiritual powers No. 3, judgement; No. 4, love; No. 7, understanding; No. 11, elimination and No. 12, life.

I relax and let myself go. I cede bitterness and wrong evaluation, unnecessary criticism and nagging to the spiritual powers of elimination. It lets it all go and makes me free. Divine love penetrates my joints and muscles. Loving understanding and tolerance renew the flow of my vital forces. I cede judgement to the divine laws of order. I am filled with perfect peace. Divine warmth penetrates my joints and muscles. I am enfolded in loving rays of warmth. I am filled with divine love, and divine understanding resolves all my conflicts in love. I feel the divine stream flowing through my arteries; I feel healing and cleansing flowing through me. New life and divine love and understanding fill my body, soul and spirit.

Anorexia nervosa:

The spiritual cause of anorexia nervosa—extreme loss of weight—lies in the following conflict: you are greedily seeking something in your life but you are afraid of the responsibility involved. Thus, you are reluctant to leave girlhood behind and step into adulthood. You reject womanhood and your periods will also be irregular for a long time. On the one hand, you yearn desperately for love and security and, on the other, you are afraid of what they involve. The symbolic result is that you vomit, or spit out, this secret love after every meal because your mind rejects it and, in consequence, your stomach cannot tolerate it. You even stick your finger down your throat so that you are forced to be sick (the symbol of disgust). I often also meet anorexia among women who married too young, had several children and then, one day, fell in love with another man. However, since they soon became unable to cope with this double life, either in their own eyes or in regard to their husbands and children, they wasted away until no more than a skeleton remained. The day they realized where they really belonged and their sense of responsibility slowly began to develop, they could be cured. We must, therefore, seek the happy medium, that is to say we have to learn that we must often forego the things we greedily pursue in life, for life teaches us that we cannot have everything we want in this world.

Ask yoursef in a moment of quiet: Where is the cause of my conflict

2

2

Exercise:

Mobilize the spiritual powers No. 1, faith; No. 4, love and No. 10, initiative.

The power of faith strengthens my body, soul and spirit. All my secret fears are dissolved by the power of divine order that channels my life in the right path. I am filled with divine light and am capable from now on of mastering my life in divine love, full of courage and enthusiasm. Divine initiative pervades me and gives me responsibility that I can carry. I am filled with peace and light.

Insomnia (sleeplessness):

Insomnia is far more common in those countries where materialism predominates, especially in the towns, than it is in the country and the mountains, or in the so-called under—or undeveloped countries. The addiction to every kind of sleeping-pill is far more widespread than we are prepared to admit. The spiritual causes of insomnia are a lack of primeval confidence, hidden depression, fear of the night, of being alone, a not wanting to let go, a refusal to come to terms with the dark. In other words you lack the ability to surrender to the dark and the night. You can change this state of affairs through a conscious effort to reconcile yourself with the law of night and the dark, by accepting it, surrendering to it in the same way you surrender to daytime and daylight; by slowly developing a sense of security, liberated from your broodings and able to steer your thoughts along positive lines. If the partner in your life is beside you, a satisfying act of love in which you surrender in complete confidence will always be the best soporific! Love is a universal cure so long as it is genuine, joyous and giving.

Exercise:

Mobilize the spiritual powers No. 1, faith; No. 4, love; No. 7, understanding; No. 9, order and No. 11, elimination.

I am completely calm and relaxed. I am completely calm and relaxed. Divine love enfolds me and affords me warmth and security. All the relationships and affairs in my life are ordered by divine love. My fears leave me. I eliminate them, for God is in me and helps me. I am not alone. I feel that I am under divine protection and guidance. I love the night and the darkness and communion with you, O Lord. I love your presence which fills me with confidence. I am borne up by your divine love and understanding and filled with a perfect ability to surrender to the night. I lay my sleep in your hands, knowing that you are watching over me. You, O Lord, are the source of my primeval confidence. You are my love, strength, truth and life, my light and my joy.

Accidents and Broken Bones:

The spiritual reason for accidents and fractures is your wanting to live your life too fast.

Accidents: you have erred from your path, you have lost control and, having once started to skid, you have gone off the road (probably in a bend where you failed to see the straight, the "honest" way!). Or you were no longer able to brake because you are in general too tempestuous and always go at things like a bull at a gate.

Bone fractures: your broken limb gives you the opportunity of lying quietly in bed and thinking about the "break" in your life, to finish, or break with the past and to achieve a breakthrough to a new, blessed and successful future. But for the time being you are hindered in your activities and your movement because you have exaggerated and must now bend your mind to moderation.

Fractures of the pelvis often occur in older people who have always dominated their families and whose gradually failing strength prevents them from continuing to do this. It means that the change is breaking you.

Exercise:

Mobilize the spiritual powers No. 1, faith; No. 4, love and No. 9, order.

I am filled with tranquillity and peace. All that lies behind me belongs to the past, all error and confusion is set to rights by the spiritual power of order. Divine love allows me to live in the present and points the way to a blessed and successful future. I am once again filled with divine life and am able to appreciate this. I believe in the effect of divine wisdom, truth and love.

Cancer (Tumours)—Ulcers:

There are many spiritual causes for the universal disease, cancer, which we healers also call "frozen love". In a book on medicine written by a cancer research worker I once read that 75% of cancer cases are due to incorrect nutrition, the immoderate consumption of pills and drugs, nicotine and alcohol, the use of toxic cosmetics and to the general toxicity of the environment. 30% are caused by wrong thinking and acting and are also the result of inner conflicts and contradictions, of our innumerable and unnecessary fears which are aggravated by the media, by the heartbreak caused by the loss of a loved one, by psychological shock and long-standing states of tension arising from struggles for power between married couples, in families and in social and business life. Other reasons are general stress, errors in upbringing, disappointment, egoism, impatience, resentment, hate, envy and jealousy.

It has already been mentioned that the heart is the only organ exempt from attack by cancer. Why is this? Because the heart is the seat of love. Heart means love, feeling, unity with others, positive thinking, gratitude for everything, acceptance. "Frozen" love can always be

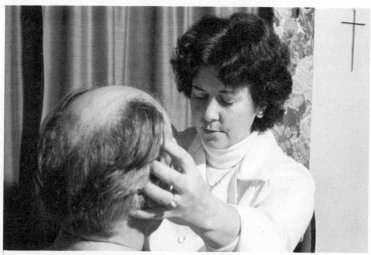

Madeleine giving spiritual healing treatment in Switzerland.

thawed out—it is never too late to defrost! It must always be remembered that cancer can quickly be made to disappear by the simple expedient of the positive use of thought and feeling, a genuine "seeing of the light" and profound gratitude and by the giving of much love and assurance. In his book, *The Spiritual Power of Healing within Us*, Dr. Masaharu Taniguchi of Japan describes how many cases of cancer have been cured by this becoming aware of the error of one's ways, this "seeing of the light", and by a subsequent change in one's way of thinking and feeling. It cannot be over-emphasized that hate, resentment and feelings of aversion and distaste cause an abnormal secretion of hormones in our internal organs which in turn leads to a subconscious lessening of resistance of the organism to disease—and I speak from twenty-three years of experience. Never forget that hate, resentment, envy, jealousy and unnecessary, harsh criticism violate conformity of the consciousness with the immutable laws and, ultimately, damage no one but yourself. For that which you sow you shall also reap. Therefore, go to work on yourself in a positive sense every day in all that you think, speak and do; you owe this to your body, your spirit and your soul.

I have often known women who, for some reason or other, suddenly started hating their husbands, their uppermost wish being to hit out at them with their fists—whereby the husband was generally not responsible for the change in his wife's behaviour. And what happened? A fist-sized tumour developed in the woman's lower abdomen: in her imagination the woman had hit her husband dozens of times and her thoughts had become embodied in herself. However, the spiritual cause of tumours can also be the need for an increase in understanding for someone close—for example, in the case just described, the woman should develop the spiritual powers of faith, strength and gratitude. She will have to learn to renew her confidence in her husband, to give him spiritual support and to stand by him with counsel and active aid. Should he have changed his profession or his place of employment, she must develop a genuine sense of gratitude and step out along this new path with him, full of courage, towards a different but nonetheless interesting future.

I have also known women who were greatly attached to their husbands and still developed myoma in the uterus. In the course of searching conversation it transpired that they harboured a secret desire for a baby or even several children but, since there was an agreement between the couple concerning family planning, these women were forced to repress their secret yearnings. The myoma represented the children they secretly wished for and were the direct consequence of their unfulfilled desires. A forty-year-old woman, the mother of three children, once said to me, "Oh, Mrs. Riedel! What I really wanted was seven more children." And seven myoma formed in her uterus. Thus, myoma, tumours and cysts—so long as they are not too big—can be brought to disappear as quickly as they came through a change of thinking, above all when the sufferer can talk things over with someone they trust. A woman who came to me with a myoma the size of a child's head in her uterus—and whom I was forced to send to hospital for its removal—"spiritually" experienced the "secret birth" of the child she had subconsciously desired and was happy to have been able to "bear a child" at least in spirit. Yes, we women are quite simply sensitive creatures with tender feelings and strange, secret desires. I am certainly no exception! So I shall tell you a story of something that happened to me less than two years ago, something that both my children and my son-in-law knew about. After their marriage my daughter and her husband lived with me for a short time until they were able to set themselves up in their own home. Upon the birth of their first baby, Sandra, my joy was such that an abnormally high hormone secretion resulted and milk flowed into my breasts as if I myself were a young mother! I could have breast-fed the little girl for many weeks, such was the source of supply, and I was forced to resort to a pump. In spirit, I had shared the period of gestation and the birth of little Sandra so intensely it was as if I had been delivered of her myself. Since I have a deep love for children, this is perhaps not all that surprising. I was forty-two at the time and people called me things like the "original grandmother" or the "pseudo-mother".

In cases of abortion I have known many women experience the "spiritual birth" of their child. Numerous women and young girls have even "seen" these unborn children growing up. In the case of sensitive women there is the danger that, as "penitence" for their "sin" they subconsciously maimed themselves in that they subsequently underwent one operation after another. This is, of course, a wrong and dangerous path which leads to self-destruction. You will be aware that the reasons for this step were many, varied and frequently very serious. You cannot change matters. But you can honestly forgive yourself and in future accept what your Creator gives you. And you can consciously make good that which has caused you so much suffering, directly by your attitude towards those you meet or, indirectly, through co-operation with charitable organizations.

Exercises in cases of Cancer:

Mobilize all the spiritual powers: faith, strength, judgement, love, power, imagination, understanding, will-power, order, initiative, elimination and life.

Divine light is all about me, giving me the strength of intuitive understanding. the divine love of Christ liberates me from all the errors of the past, from disharmony and disunion. I feel the forgiving love of Christ within me. There is no reason to condemn myself and others since in future I shall be borne up and strengthened by divine love. Divine understanding permits me to live in peace with all those around me. Harmony fills my heart and I am able to transmit divine love to others. I have confidence in myself and those around me. We are filled with divine light and love. God has made me perfect therefore no sickness can exist in me. Divine love heals me and renews all my cells, glands, nerves and organs. Divine strength encompasses my ego. The rays of divine strength flow through my body, my spirit and my soul. In me is deep faith, divine love, divine understanding, divine order, divine strength, divine judgement, divine power, divine imagination and the divine will to recover, divine courage, divine elimination and divine life. I am divine light and divine peace.

I should like to conclude this chapter with a quotation from the Apocrypha about wisdom (*Ecclesiasticus* 1:11-20):

"The fear of the Lord is honour, and glory, and gladness, and a crown of rejoicing.

The fear of the Lord maketh a merry heart, and giveth joy, and gladness, and a long life.

Whoso feareth the Lord, it shall go well with him at the last, and he shall find favour in the day of his death.

To fear the Lord is the beginning of wisdom: and it was created with the faithful in the womb.

She hath built an everlasting foundation with men, and she shall continue with their seed.

To fear the Lord is fullness of wisdom, and filleth me with her fruits.

She filleth all their house with things desirable, and the garners with her increase.

The fear of the Lord is a crown of wisdom, making peace and perfect health to flourish; both which are the gifts of God: and it enlargeth their rejoicing that love him.

Wisdom raineth down skill and knowledge of understanding, and exalteth them to honour that hold her fast.

The root of wisdom is to fear the Lord, and the branches thereof are long life."

III. Reports and Contributions

Report by the spiritual healer, Tom Johanson, England

THE SPIRITUALIST ASSOCIATION OF GREAT BRITAIN
The Largest Spiritualist Association in the World
Established 1872   Incorporated 1905

The Mechanics of Spiritual Healing

Somewhere I read that "a new power is growing throughout the world". It would be more correct to say that *knowledge* of this ancient power (spiritual healing) is growing throughout the world. The power itself is as old as mankind.

Though Great Britain has made remarkable advances in adopting spiritual healing socially, professionally and by nationally establishing practices which make spiritual healing freely and generally available to the public, this is by no means to say that the British are especially blessed with this miraculous healing force. Although it is true that spiritual healers are allowed to work in nearly 2,000 hospitals, that many doctors openly apply spiritual healing and it is frequently demonstrated on television and written about in national magazines and newspapers, it is only the *knowledge* that has been more readily accepted by the British nation.

The healing force is of the *spirit*. That is, it emanates from the vital source of *all* human life called *spiritual*. This power of healing is available within *all* persons—no matter what their nationality—who are not totally attached to a materialistic way of life. It manifests itself only when complete co-operation, or attunement, between would-be healer and the inner spiritual being is attained. We hear about schools for the training of healers but there is no such school on earth at which this co-operation, or spiritual attunement, can be taught. Of course, we have to accept that this entire earth life is one big school in which the sole aim is to teach everyone how (voluntarily or involuntarily) to achieve a sense of spiritual awareness; to teach that Man is essentially an eternal, and therefore indestructible spiritual being that has taken on physical form for a limited period of time. All our daily experiences, especially the painful ones, are designed by spiritual law to reveal to us the limitations, or illusions of matter.

As far back into the history of Man as we can go there have always been certain people who had the power to heal. Some cured pain and disease by simply placing their hands upon the affected part. Others used an extraordinary knowledge of herbal potions. Some used prayers and incantations frequently accompanied by complex rituals associated with thier religious beliefs. Many of these techniques worked but in all instances there has been a common human factor—the establishment of a spiritual rapport, or attunement, with the sick person. Spiritual rapport cannot be disassociated from compassion, or love.

Throughout history medical scientists have laughed at unorthodox forms of healing but however illogical the form of treatment appeared to the "trained" practitioner, it is now abundantly obvious to observers in most countries all over the world that permanent, sometimes miraculous cures have been and are still being achieved by practitioners who use nothing more than a sense of caring and a spiritual bond.

The spiritual healer is a sensitive and realistic therapist. He has no ambitions whatsoever to replace the orthodox medical man or surgeon. The good healer recognizes these medical therapists as indispensable workers vital to the welfare of the community. However, the healer has (or should have) a deep awareness of the spiritual nature of Man and it is only through this understanding that he endeavours to restore inner harmony and emotional balance where there is sickness or dis-ease. This the dedicated healer frequently achieves without drugs, surgery or mechanical diagnostic aids, relying solely on the natural sources of spiritual energy that lie within us and recognizing that this source of energy, from which all healing derives, is of God. All true healers will agree that love is the only power behind all healing.

The reaction of love, a sense of compassion when witnessing sickness immediately brings the spirit and the physical body into a state of perfect attunement but, strange to relate, we have no knowledge of the exact nature of this healing energy nor of the mechanics of how it applies itself. To attempt to analyze spiritual processes would necessitate translation into a language totally unknown to and beyond the comprehension of the human intellect. We can speak only in terms of achieving a "higher consciousness"—a language known only to the evolved occultist or the adept of deep meditation.

There are various types of healing which, generally speaking, can be divided into four main categories:

1. Spiritual healing
2. Spirit operations
3. Magnetic healing
4. Divine healing

Spiritual Healing:

Here the healer believes that his healing actions are a combination of attunement with his inner spiritual consciousness and that which is inspired outside his own consciousness. The power he is transmitting is of himself but his actions are directed and sometimes fully controlled by intelligences other than his own. He is frequently aware through psychic sensitivity of the presence of guiding entities and it is through their instructions that he is able to direct healing forces to the patient. In addition the healer is able to receive instructions concerning the nature of the problem.

Because of these guiding entities, most healers are capable of treating patients from a distance without any physical contact with the sick person. Attunement with the outside entities is made either through the process of prayer, meditation or psychic contact. It is even possible for a person to receive healing without any knowledge that treatment is taking place. During spiritual healing spinal curvatures will frequently straighten under the healer's hands; prolapsed disc, goitre and duodenal ulcers will yield to spiritual healing almost immediately.

Spirit Operations:

Where the healer is capable of going into a state of trance and his physical body is controlled by an outside spirit entity, this form of healing is referred to as a spirit operation. The entranced healer stands over the patient, who is lying fully conscious upon a bed, and diagnoses the nature of the disease. If the disease is such that would normally respond to classical surgery, than an "etheric operation" is immediately carried out. If the controlling spirit had been a doctor or surgeon on earth, then he goes through precisely the same actions as if he were doing an ordinary operation. In other words he would appear to use scalpels and go through cutting procedures. Later, after the operation, he will go through the actions of sewing up the patient's body. Patients frequently feel a mild sensation of cutting, the introduction of a hyperdermic needle and the sewing up. Sometimes red swellings appear where the operation was carried out. This is sometimes accompanied by some soreness. However difficult it may be for us to accept these operations, many people have made remarkable recoveries and there is considerable evidence to support these claims.

Magnetic Healing:

The magnetic healer believes that an abundance of healing energies are stored in his body. He therefore uses healing passes to control magnetic fluctuations within the patient's body. Certain passes are used to stimulate certain parts and others to soothe or calm down. The healer thinks of his hands as magnets and as he passes them over the body he senses parts that are magnetized and others that are not. In this way he obtains his diagnoses. It is believed that the non-magnetized parts are diseased. Some healers use pendulums for the same purpose. Magnetic healers also use radiesthesia or "diagnostic boxes". It is claimed that, by using a drop of blood or human hairs, emanations from disease can be measured.

Divine Healing:

The divine healer is often a devoted Christian and a very orthodox churchgoer. He believes that only through the direct intervention of Jesus Christ will healing take place. The doctrine of the forgiveness of sin is very strong. The patient is then led to believe that his sickness is the direct consequence of his unbelief in Christian precepts. If a cure does not take place, then it is believed that God has not yet forgiven the sinner. If failure follows failure, then this could have a very serious effect upon the patient's mind and consequently on his physical body.

For a spiritual healer to have any idea of healing he must have a thorough understanding not only of disease but also of its origin and before he can achieve that he must have a complete understanding of Man himself. He must not think of man as just a physical body. Man exists on a wide variety of levels of consciousness. There is the physical or material level; the psycho-electrical level which is very closely connected with the physical body. Then there is the emotional level, the intellectual, psychic and mystical spiritual levels. I use the word "mystical" because we know that there are many levels of spiritual consciousness but we are aware of only a very few. Even though many of these levels are beyond the awareness of many people, they still have a direct influence on our general health. Each of these levels *must* be thought of as varying frequencies of energy among which there is a never-ending interplay, interaction and reaction. Physical changes manifest themselves immediately or over a period of time when there is a sudden change or frequent alterations or imbalances in the emotional or physical levels of energy. In a normally healthy person these different levels of energy function in a state of harmony while dis-ease appears as the result of a constant or frequent underlying state of disharmonious interplay.

The act of healing implies the restoring of the state of balance among the levels of consciousness. But first the healer must be capable of identifying the area of imbalance, removing the disturbing forces and then, by contact healing and conversation, establishing the best mental conditions under which the *inner system* of self-healing will operate. It is of the utmost importance for healers and patients to remember that this state of inner balance, or process of disturbance between the various levels, is a two-way action. In other words, there is not only a psychosomatic element in disease but a physio-psychic process as well.

This means that not only is a disharmonious mind capable of disrupting the natural, normal operation of the body (as seen, for example, in the appearance of stomach ulcers, high blood pressure, fainting attacks, tension, blushing caused by embarrassment, racing pulses, sweating caused by fear etc.) but also that the body is capable of creating certain disturbing mental states such as pre-menstrual tension, menapause and the over-activity of those suffering from hyperthyroidism etc.

Spiritual healing requires no apparatus or special training; only the *spiritual* desire (otherwise, compassion) to help the sick. The power to heal comes from the higher aspects of the mind. This higher mind attracts other spiritual personalities, or helping spirits, who are also anxious to heal the sick. They are capable of transmitting helpful, guiding, inspirational thoughts to the healer which is why no healer need ever worry about what is the best technique for him to use. Always be guided by your inspirational thoughts since they come from a higher form of intelligence. There is no healing power in the techniques themselves. Healing can be performed from a distance. Healing can never take place *out* of time. When a healer first meditates and concentrates upon certain patients then, when he is asleep, he may consciously or unconsciously travel to the patient. Patients can also receive healing from a distance when the healer sits down in meditation and consciously concentrates on his patients. There need not be any physical contact and the patient need not be made aware that healing is being sent him.

Innumerable tests and observations have been made by medical scientists and psychical researchers on the work of spiritual healers and the results thereof. Although the healing energy cannot be analyzed, it has been observed and recorded. It has been conclusively proved that when a healer lays his hands on a patient a positive flow of energy, capable of correcting a physical problem, takes place. It is known, however, that the energy is an independent intelligence far greater than our own. To prove this, some years ago a group of scientists wanted to record the energy that flows from my hands while I am healing. After fixing the necessary electrodes to my hands and placing a patient in the chair, I began to concentrate. Unfortunately there was no reaction whatever. After rechecking the apparatus there was still no reaction. When we decided to change the patient there was an immediate response from the apparatus—*the healing energy had recognized immediately that the first person was perfectly healthy.*

The entire history of spiritual healing is replete with scientific records proving over and over again that there is a definite emanation of an undefinable but potent energy which is not only a super-intelligence but also has the power entirely to remove or greatly to reduce the source of illness. Apart from contact healing, we have been able to witness the effects of the energy waves when transmitted to a patient over many miles and the resultant phenomena have conclusively proved that distance has no effect whatsoever on the healing power of this energy.

In conclusion, let me state that we have more than enough conclusive evidence to prove that within each of us, in unlimited quantities, lies this divine power to heal the sick. Therefore let each one of us determine so to live our lives and discipline our thoughts as to be ever conscious of this divine, unifying power which forever rests within the heart of us but will flow only when a cry for help is heard by the love in our hearts. Just as electricity—potently present everywhere—becomes effective only in the presence of a conductor, so spiritual power becomes effective only in the presence of a person who is aware of the divine law. The healing power of saints is not for a select few but is a general, human experience.

Extract from the Report by Dr. Arthur Massena.

President of the

SOCIEDADE DE MEDECINA E ESPIRITISMO DO RIO DE JANEIRO

Paranormal Phenomenology—Scientific Research

During its forty-two years of research, examinations and treatments the "Sociedade de Medecina e Espiritismo do Rio de Janeiro" (Medical and Spiritist Society, Rio de Janeiro) has identified and studied thirty-one different pathological phenomena and spiritual treatments.

The "Sociedade de Medecina e Espiritismo do Rio de Janeiro" was founded on 11th June, 1941 and celebrated its 42nd anniversary by publishing this account of the thirty-one paranormal, pathological phenomena and the modes of treating them which it had discovered or identified in the course of its unremitting scientific studies.

Washing the Subconsciousness:

The human spirit consists of the *consciousness* whose function it is to capture, immediately or through study, in the form of knowledge or experience, everything which exists or appears outside the body; of the *subconsciousness,* the seat of memory, which continuously records the knowledge acquired and recalls it to the person's consciousness whenever necessary, in the form of memories; and of the *unconsciousness* where all the knowledge and experience acquired in the course of the various lives (incarnations), be they of an intellectual or moral character, are finally integrated into the structure of the personality and, in their turn—whenever necessary and independent of the human will—surface into the consciousness. The unconsciousness is also the seat of all automatism or self-action, be it intellectual, moral or connected with the function of the human organism. Since it records everything, that which is both good and bad for the person concerned, it can become necessary to drive out from the unconsciousness all self-action that could harm the person, including any "tricks". This can be done only through a *washing of the unconsciousness* in which human magnetism and prayer are used alternately. It is transmitted by placing the left hand on the medium's forehead (in this way the spirit to be treated is reached via the medium) and by desiring fervently that the spirit remove from the subconscious anything that confuses, disquietens and brings disadvantage, rather in the manner of a dry, constant vomiting. This should continue until there is nothing left to eliminate. The psychoanalytical cartharsis thus triggered by oral suggestion causes retrogression from the present to the time of birth, while the washing of the unconsciousness by the magnetic leading back of the personality encompasses this life and as much as is necessary of preceding incarnations.

Report by Mr. G. Schumacher, clergyman and psychologist, Wald, Zurich.

Spiritual healing and becoming whole

In my study, a very depressive young woman sits across from me. Her eyes express a sense of hopelessness. And yet there is within her a hidden hope—otherwise she would not have come. She has been given psychiatric drugs, which have helped her only temporarily. Now she wants to start with psychotherapy. We are working on her dreams and imagination. After a number of meetings, we start to touch on a mysterious deeper dimension in her life, her own religious world. For the first time, she consciously comes face to face with the divine element, transcending all else, and she feels God working within her as a power which after weeks and months of joylessness and apathy gives her once more hope in a new future. At this instant, I understand that we must delve deeper in our therapy than we normally find it necessary to do. What we notice first is often a physical symptom: stomach pains, throat pains, back pains, problems of sight, and many others, but behind most of these things there lies a trouble of the soul, for there is no doubt that the soul tries to make itself heard through the body. If we follow this track, we may perhaps reach a bitter experience that this person has had in childhood and which has put the life of the soul out of balance. Sometimes the symptoms touch the life of the soul with greater immediacy—in that the person suffers from neurotic sleeping problems or from lingering depression. It is not always helpful to search into the past of a human being for possible causes—sometimes we must remain in the present, but then delve deeper in this dimension. Is this person happy in his family life, or in his work? Does he really live his life to the full, or does he merely vegetate? What creative gifts lie within him unawakened? What is the sense and the aim of his life? With questions such as these, we have crossed a scarcely perceivable frontier into a land where a human being is faced with his deeper relationship with the divine, with his religion. I do not of course mean by this his relationship with any particular religious denomination, but rather his real resting place—something which people do not often express openly but in which they must nevertheless live their whole existence.

These questions lead us into the spiritual sphere, which plays an important role in the therapeutical process. For human beings consist not only of body and soul, but also of spirit. The spirit is the real living thing, the giver of life, and without it the body is nothing but inanimate matter. On the other hand, the spirit can very well exist without the body. The spirit has created the body as a tool with which it can do its work in this world. If a hammer slips from the hand of its master and acts independently, then its activities may lead to disaster. It is only in the hand of its master that a tool can do the work for which it is designed.

The spirit is the eternal, the divine, which realises itself in the material world—which brings spirituality to the material world. In his inner being, therefore, the human being has something of the divine. If he has lost the vital link to this divine core, to the spirit, then his body and his soul will become sick. If a human being is no longer in harmony with the life-force within him, his soul and his body lose their equilibrium. So if we want to help the sick human being in a comprehensive way, we must learn to see him once more as a whole: as body, soul and spirit. It is not enough to come to grips with symptoms: it is far more important that the human being should be healed in his spiritual dimension. Jesus came to earth to help mankind to achieve precisely this. He saw that, though human beings were still bound together with each other in the institutional sense, they had lost their living link to the divine spirit and had thus become sick. Before he healed the man suffering from palsy, he said: "Thy sins are forgiven thee." (*Matthew* 9: 2). He was not referring to the evil deeds of a particular person, but to the fact that his links with God had been broken. He was referring to his inner disunity. As Jesus acted upon him, God returned to his being. This outward experience started something within him which was decisive: spiritual force once again found its entrance to the divine centre within him, was once again in unison with his innermost being. In this way, his body was also healed, because in the most absolute sense his life was healed.

Today, we are faced with the same important task of bringing human beings back into contact with God—and this is not something which must happen in a particular place, it must happen within a person. It is particularly urgent today because human beings who have fallen away from their inner harmony can cause catastrophes not only in this world but in the universe itself. It is urgently necessary that we should again become aware that in our existence we must put spirit before body, and not vice versa.

Two thousand years ago, the Essenes tried in their daily meditations to bring the heavenly Father and Mother earth into unison in order constantly to increase their forces. They knew that their real existence was in the spiritual world and that their bodies existed only as an instrument with which they should work here on earth. Their spiritual exercises helped them not only to maintain excellent health but also to possess extraordinary powers as healers, therapists, seers, teachers etc. How far we are today from this! And yet we may not be as far away as we think, for the spirit lives in everyone of us. In other words we are part of the spirit, and we have a divine future. Through all our incarnations, we have only one aim: to find our way back to God. As long as we live on this earth, it is our task to help the divine spirit to be realised. This is the hardest task which is given to us human beings, for the greatest obstacle preventing the realisation of the spirit within us is not so much our exterior circumstances as our interior primitive ego. The divine spirit can only realise itself in our lives when this ego is ready to give up its place, which means to die. Many human beings fight desperately all their lives long against death, instead of letting themselves go, in the realisation that every one of us has to die. Many corporal illnesses, and many diseases of the soul are signs of this desperate resistance to spiritual rebirth. C. G. Jung called this rebirth "self-realisation", and Paul described it in his *Epistle to the Galatians* (2:20) in these terms: "Yet not I, but Christ liveth in me." Whatever words we choose, it is a question of breaking through to the divine in the midst of our earthly life. It is a matter of our being able to say: "Not mine, but thy will be done." When our own lives have become healed in this sense, then we can also heal other people. It is a sign of the distance from God at which we find ourselves in our Western Christian society that the healing power is granted to only one professional group, the doctors. The implication is that "healing" can be brought about through one kind of theoretical and scientific training only. Yet it is true that every person has healing powers within himself, because he is part of the spirit. If I make myself aware of this and go about the use of these powers in a responsible way, I can contribute to the general healing process on our planet. It is certainly true that there do exist some extraordinarily gifted people who are specially called upon to heal. But we must not close our eyes to the fact that we are all part of the divine spirit, and we can all help in the healing process of this "groaning and travailing creation" (*Romans* 8: 19-23). Chirst said: "He that believeth in me, the works that I do shall he do also: and greater works than these shall he do." (*John* 14: 12). Provided that we understand that this "belief" is not simply a repetition of institutionalised teaching, but rather the living experience of Christ, the divine working within us, then today also the spirit is able to work miracles through every single one of us.

Contribution from Dr. Walter A. Frank, Schloss Vehn, D-5483 Sinzig

Healers, Healing, Being and Remaining Whole

Lately, alternative and spiritual healing procedures are becoming increasingly popular, even within the medical profession. Although in the health field the highest precept should be, "Whatever heals is good", there is nevertheless resistance, if not hostility in the medical establishment towards any method of healing which deviates from classical, medical craft. Yet even in modern physics a radical change has taken place in the interpretation of the nature of matter, i.e. matter is described as a special form of vibration of spacetime. Spacetime is a very abstract notion and may equally well be interpreted as a special form of the cosmic spirit. Thus, physicists such as Jean E. Charon, Schopper of CERN and Burkhard Hewin speak of matter as a special phenomenon of spirit. Living systems are a particularly sophisticated form of matter since they consist of highly differentiated molecules. Now, if matter—elementary matter—can be described as a form of spirit, this should be all the more valid for an exceedingly complex composition of matter. And if matter—bodily matter—is spirit in its intrinsic nature, what about the attempts to regulate malfunctions of such systems by spiritual means? What about spiritual healing? Is it not high time for some juridical reforms concerning this subject which is of such great importance for the well-being of humankind? Should not spiritual means of healing be even more promising than the classical allopathic methods which are based purely on a materialistic paradigm, even if this very paradigm be overcome by physics in the meantime.

With or without valid laws, spiritual healing is practised wellnigh throughout the world, and with remarkable success. Most of the patients that come to spiritual healers are those that have been given up by classical medicine as hopeless. And many of them can be cured against all allopathic probability. And those that cannot be cured can either be alleviated or the attitude of the sufferers towards their illness changed to the positive—which is already a help in its own way. These facts speak for themselves and are the reason for the rapidly spreading information about the possibilities of spiritual healing. Notwithstanding, the resistance of the medical lobby is understandable since the nature of the spiritual approach to illness and health is radically different from the classical, medical one as it is based on an entirely different paradigm. And this applies for the "patient" as well as for the "healer". A change in attitude is nevertheless at present taking place, at least in Britain. After H.R.H. Prince Charles suggested, while addressing the British Medical Association, that "spiritual healing be dealt with a bit more thoroughly and intelligently", spiritual healing has infiltrated government hospitals where patients can ask for a spiritual healer to supplement the regular medical treatment in co-operation with the doctors. In the meantime more than 2,000 hospitals have introduced this practice, obviously with success since it is rapidly spreading. Also the media—even in such backward countries as the Federal Republic of Germany, are about to change their attitude towards spiritual healing and related practices from the ironical to the more serious. Thus, it seems that matters are taking a turn for the better. As usual, however, the juridical establishment is the most backward in coming forward and, in most Western countries, the laws are still against helping the suffering by a spiritual approach towards health and sickness. Let us hope for an improvement in this respect as well—for the benefit of all those in need of spiritual treatment.

And this need is great. In most cases those who come to a spiritual healer have a long record of suffering, having gone from one doctor to another and from hospital to hospital. All they are told in the end is that the only thing to do is to get accustomed to their suffering and learn to live with it. Generally, the spiritual healer is really their very last hope. And in many cases they find help there. And even if they cannot be helped physically, they at least obtain an introduction to the nature of their condition which is entirely different from any they could get from a materialistically orientated medical practitioner: they learn to find the deeper cause of their suffering, which may even have something to do with previous incarnations—a notion unknown to the materialistic world's interpretation. Usually even those who cannot be cured by spiritual healing at least experience a change of attitude towards life and alleviation of their suffering. Often they outlive by months, if not years, the time accorded them by the medical profession. Whatever the outcome of spiritual treatment may be, it will never produce any negative side effects as is so often the case with conventional treatment by means of drugs, radiation and surgery. And this is because spiritual healing is based on a fundamentally different conception of physical and spiritual reality.

In this conception the body and its functions are secondary, the spiritual counterparts (astral body, spirit body) are primary. Indeed, the physical body is only a replica of the spiritual "entelechy" on the material plane of reality, which is itself of a spiritual nature but on a different level of vibration—modern physics tell us just the same! Therefore, spiritual healing in no way interferes with the material body and its functions—as classical medicine has to do—but approaches solely the spiritual counterparts, regulating the flow of transcendental energies and restoring the balance and harmony within the spiritual system of a person in the hope that it will "materialize" on the physical plane—which it does if the treatment is successful. And successful it is in at least as many cases as classical medicine can claim! But, because of the way it works, spiritual healing is the ideal complementary approach to the medical one and optimal results could be expected by combining the two—as is recently being done in Great Britain with excellent success. It is warmly recommended that other countries copy this example!

Sceptics have often claimed that such "miraculous" cures are the result of "belief", "auto-suggestion" and "self-fulfilling prophecy". The author of these lines has studied the disciplines of sociology and psychology, relevant for such interpretations, at university level and knows what he is talking about. He has also experienced the literally instant healing by a Lhamo (lady shaman) in the Himalayas of a viral bronchitis (infections are not susceptible to "suggestions" and the like!). It vanished in the twinkling of an eye (dematerialized) and the energy lost after five weeks of suffering was restored equally instantly and permanently. Such effects cannot be explained by "psychological" arguments. They can well be explained within the much wider framework of the spiritual paradigm and its holistic logics. And within this paradigm even "exotic" phenomena can be explained, such as the "surgery" of the Brazilian healer, Arigo, or the bloody practices of Philippine "logurgics" who push their bare hands through the skin into the bowels and extract all sorts of peculiar tissues, with blood flowing in abundance.

Now comes the argument of classical medicine that a cure is not a cure if it cannot be explained how it works—at least that is the ideology. And "explanation" here means explanation in all detail. Spiritual healers will claim that it is not they at all who do the job but that they are only a channel for the spirit entities working through them—which is, of course, a proper description of "mediumism". And, again, classical medicine will state that this is all nonsense since there is no such thing as a spiritual entity. And again those old arguments of "auto-suggestion" and the like will be pulled out of the rubbish box of the materialistic paradigm.

And yet there are members of this selfsame medical profession who have done research on precisely this problem—is there something that survives after the "death" of the body? In the meantime, the evidence brought by Drs. Moody, Stevenson, Becker, Sabom and others is piling up in abundance so that, in the face of this evidence, any self-respecting court would be forced to sentence the materialists to accept the survival hypothesis. And all those cases of near-death experience and reincarnation memories and regression analyses show the very same structure: when the body ceases to function a "something", like a field of consciousness, separates from the body and hovers for some time above the physical remains of the person and is able to see and hear what is going on and to remember everything until the "recovery" or the "reincarnation" takes place. And they all experience a sort of journey through a more or less narrow and dark "tunnel" and see a very bright light afterwards which is obviously something like a spirit entity of a "higher order". Since there are mediums that claim that "dead persons" speak or write through them, using the medium's body as an instrument, there come "descriptions" of the manner of "passing" which are literally identical to the experiences of those people brought back by medical skill. And the conditions are such that no sceptic can claim that this whole business is nothing but a gigantic fake with all the thousands and thousands of people conspiring together, the scientists included. And to cap everything, every open-minded physicist who keeps himself up-to-date in his own discipline will explain bluntly that there can hardly be any other explanation since one of the basic laws of physics makes it perfectly obvious—the law of the preservation of energy!

This law says that the total amount of energy has always to remain the same because energy can neither be created nor destroyed. All the ways of gaining energetic functions in this universe are no more than a *transfer* of energy from one kind or one level to another. Now, as nothing can be set going without energy, consciousness must obviously be some kind of energy as we set everything going by first using our consciousness. And even our body would not work, nor could we live, without our consciousness to steer our thoughts and actions. It is therefore physically compulsory that the energy of consciousness has to go somewhere when it leaves the body as a result of the latter's "death"—it cannot just vanish into thin air. And it had to come from somewhere in the first place to bring the tissues of the foetus to life. So where did it come from and where does it go? There is no great need for guesswork and speculation. We have the concrete information from those who have died but are still communicating with us through mediums and from those who can remember their last "death" and "rebirth" and from those who have almost died but were brought back to life. And, since all their information is coherent and consistent, it would be silly to go on obstinately asking the question. It would be far more intelligent to accept the reported facts.

Thus, there are people who have contact with the "other side" and communicate with such bodiless fields of consciousness—more simply called "spirits"—and who use these contacts to help people who are still in the body with their health problems. Naturally, spirits must have wider and better experience and knowledge about certain conditions within this intermediate field of existence between perfect physical health (what is that, by the way?) and the breakdown of the physical organism to the state we call "death". They can see not only the atoms and molecules of bodily matter but also their spiritual counterparts on other levels of energetic vibrations and will thus have far better means of "repair" than any medical doctor can possibly ever have. And very often these healing spirits were once doctors themselves on the physical plane. All the better—this makes them doubly expert on illness and health now that they are working from the spirit plane in the direction of the physical one.

Considering all these facts not a single argument can be found against the practice of spiritual healing. On the contrary, all the agruments speak for it:

1. Basically there is no such thing as "incurability" as far as spiritual healing is concerned. There is hope even for the absolutely "hopeless" cases.

2. No side effects are possible since no "remedies" are used, nor is there any physical impact on the body of the "patient". This may sound paradoxical but it is so in spite of the "surgery" practised by spiritual healers since they "operate" only on the astral or spirit body—with an illusionary "image", as if the hands of the healer were penetrating the tissues of the body! (In fact, here, only spirit penetrates spirit.)

3. Spiritual healing follows not only a spiritual but also a holistic principle; thus, spiritual healing always "works" on the whole of the organism-mind-spirit unity and not reductionistically on parts of the body system. That is, the ailment is "found", wherever its cause may

be located physically or psychically. And that also means that

4. no "wrong diagnosis" is possible since the diagnosis, however it may be produced, is of no importance for the curing process because it is always the entire system that is "treated", regulating its imbalances and dysfunctions. And thus

5. there are no "wrong methods" in spiritual healing because all the "procedures" have only a symbolic, ritualistic nature and do not actually interfere with anything physical within the "patient's" body system. They "work" only on the "astral" and/or "spirit" counterpart of the body. Therefore, there can be

6. no interference with parallel medical treatment. On the contrary,

7. spiritual and medical treatment are complementary and call for creative co-operation for the sake of the suffering whose healing should be the ultimate aim of all endeavours within the health services—that is what they are there for!

Let us hope that even the legislators will sooner or later (preferably sooner) come to understand this and the politicians will quickly follow to approve and implement new laws.

Article by Dr. Hans Endres, Germany

Healing—Salvation—Sanctification

Healing of the body and mind, through salvation of the soul, by sanctification in the spirit.

Paracelsus, one of the greatest doctors of all time, said: "All illness is rooted in the spirit." By using the word "spirit", he did not mean, as would be the case today, intellect or intelligible thought, but rather the original sense of God's spirit, the higher consciousness. So he wanted to say that the real root of all illness comes about through failure to appreciate the spirit of God —or in other words illness comes about through false consciousness. It can be deduced from this that healing is the equivalent of putting false consciousness to rights by bringing true knowledge to bear upon it.

False consciousness arrises in the first place from *ignorance*, and this in its turn comes from either lack of information or from wrong information. These also can have two kinds of origin: intentional deception or insufficient knowledge of a specialised nature. For in the present political, economic, social and personal circumstances in which we live it is hardly possible to obtain full and true information—so that general ignorance is incredibly widespread, not only among the "masses", but also among those who are supposed to be highly educated. In particular, a one-sided over-evaluation is increasingly given to technical thinking based on the natural sciences, as against thinking based on biological and psychological truths—not to mention philosophy and religion. This means that in general many poor ignorant people cause themselves and others more or less serious health problems—and this particularly applies to those people who ought to heal and have the will to heal, but in fact do more harm than good in the long run. The damage which is done every day by allopathy, surgery, psychiatry etc. is already a sufficient subject of public controversy—but without the real root of the evil ever being uncovered.

Indeed, false consciousness comes not only from intellectual ignorance (insufficient knowledge) but above all from spiritual blindness or lack of wisdom, with the result that people identify themselves with the feelings and thoughts that come to them through the body and which stem from isolation in the Ego. They therefore lose their links to their real selves, to their own souls and to universal consciousness. This results in the "social disease" of egoism, from which we all suffer more or less, and which has as its inevitable consequence the whole range of psychosomatic illnesses—for the healthiest organism cannot in the long run support the burden of an inner life which is totally isolated and the associated difficulties in establishing contact with those without. Basically, this means that every corporal illness is psychosomatic, or in other words is caused by wrong-thinking and negative feelings (if this were not the case, we should always be ill, since the external causes of illness are ever present). For normally any organism possesses or develops sufficient defensive powers to enable it to defeat all causes of illness. It is only when we ourselves weaken or block these defensive powers by indulging in all kinds of unreasonable behaviour that it is possible for us to become ill. We cannot even catch a cold if we are not first convinced in our minds that we have a cold or if we do not in some way or other behave unreasonably!

In this respect, our language is eloquent enough: when we speak of insult, what we really mean is injury to our self-esteem, or injury to our feelings. But to injure us means precisely to make us ill, just as to blacken means to make black, to darken means to make dark etc.—and this is exactly what happens! The effect of every negative feeling is to injure our general organism and is consequently one of the primary causes of illness. When we begin not only to recognise this in theory, but really to behave according to this principle, starting with education and going on to all our dealings with each other in our daily lives, then we shall find that we have done more for the general state of health than all the external remedies and methods of healing taken together!

So as long as the basic evil of false consciousness is not removed, we cannot even talk about healing in the real sense. For the most progressive medical art can in the best of cases deal only with symptoms, or replace one kind of illness with another, but it can certainly not bring about Nietzsche's "great healthiness" in the body and the mind. As a result, today all the various types of neuroses and nervous diseases, circulatory troubles and autonomic dystony, heart disease and cancer, alcoholism and the abuse of drugs have a more devastating effect than all the plagues of the Middle Ages!

From what we have seen so far, it ought to be clear that real healing is only possible through the *salvation of the soul!* The German word for salvation also means "whole" or "complete and undivided"—you can say, for example, of an earthenware vessel that it is "whole" in this sense, meaning that it is unbroken. So we must restore to the "non-whole" of the divided, separated, ego consciousness the "wholeness" of the complete and undivided consciousness of the soul. It is only in this way that the religious expression, "the salvation of the soul", can acquire an immediately relevant and realistic meaning, as opposed to something other-worldly and irrational: a transformation from dispersal, fragmentation, conflict, estrangement and division to composure, connection, co-ordination, reconciliation and unity. The only force which can heal the body is the force which heals the mind first, in that it brings back the unity and wholeness which have been destroyed.

And here we come once again to a *twofold conception of wholeness*: the wholeness of the individual soul in itself, and its being brought into the great wholeness of the world soul. Somebody who is divided within himself cannot be really healthy. The opposition between thinking and feeling, between conscious intentions and subconscious tendencies, the struggle between opposing inclinations, between will and reluctance, between conscientiousness and domination by one's physical urges, the gap between theory and practice, between recognising and being able—all this makes our mind into a destructive battlefield, instead of a serene haven of peace, in which alone healthiness can thrive in the long run.

More important than all physical measures to nurture health is therefore basic psycho-hygiene (this can also be described as a cleansing of the mind). For even worse than the growing "pollution of the environmental world" is the far-reaching "pollution of the inner world" which is caused by wrong thinking, negative feelings, unbridled urges and impulsive, panicky acts, and which covers the "soul-mirror" of our minds with a "crust of dirt" so thick that the "pure likeness" of the God-image can no longer be reflected in it.

In exactly the same way as we wash ourselves as quickly and as thoroughly as we can whenever we feel dirty on the outside, we should also wash ourselves innerly by transferring our thoughts from the disastrous fragmentation and dispersion in our minds and giving our full and undivided attention, in the form of concentration, to the unifying salvation of the soul which restores it to its wholeness. And what this means literally is *to meditate* (*meditari* in Latin: to judge from the middle of the circle). It means that we must repose in the centre of our own being, in our true self, and from there use a "spiritual compass" which will circumscribe the "horizon" of our consciousness in concentric circles spreading out endlessly until finally the most distant of our circles fades away into infinity: our individual consciousness is then completely taken into the highest consciousness of all, the wholeness of God.

Only in this way can we finally overcome the basic evil of our divided existence: by this certitude of being part of the Godhead, with which the soul, in spite of its temporary identification with the mind and the body, has always been essentially identical. And this is the real sense of *religion*: a drawing-back, a restored connection with one's origin in God. To go from a small "whole" to become part of the greater "whole"—this is "salvation of the soul" in the truest sense of the expression!

This brings us directly to the third and last aspect of health: *sanctification in the spirit.* Even in our normal use of speech, an action is said to be "sanctified" when it has been done in a selfless or dedicated way—while things which are done in a selfish, egotistic frame of mind are said to be "unsanctified". This fact was brought out in the most radical way possible by Ekkehard in one of his sermons: "If you stumble over a stone in the right frame of mind (in the presence of God), you do more than if you take the sacrament in a selfish frame of mind!"

We can also say that something which is done out of irresponsible, superficial, short-sighted or narrow-minded motives is "unsanctified", whereas actions characterised by responsibility, carefulness, conscientiousness and other spiritual motives are taken on to a higher level of consciousness and are therefore "sanctified". The theological expression for this is *sub specie aeternitatis*, which refers to the aspect of eternity.

This is valid not only for our acts but also for our whole earthly existence. As long as we identify ourselves with our transitory form and consider all its inadequacies as "natural", then we are taken up in "the dream of mortality", and we suffer from the basic evil from which sorrow, want, illness and all other evils stem. We suffer from "having fallen away" from the consciousness of God, from being lost in isolation and loneliness (the Christian "original sin"). Only when we come to the knowledge of our true nature as "immortal soul", when we awake as "the eternal spark of God" and "return to our Father's house" from "alienation" can we say that we have been finally cured and that our health has been regained.

Consequently, both Jesus and the Prophets admonished us over and over again to *rethink*, to be converted (the Greek word is *metanoia*, which has been falsely translated as "atonement"). Naturally, self-examination and, where necessary, change of direction are part of the process, because in order to be able to establish that we are travelling along the wrong path we must first pause and reflect. Only when we have realised our mistake shall we turn round as fast as possible and search for the right path—for in just the same way as it is impossible to go in two different directions at the same time, it is impossible to be at one and the same time conscious of God and attached to material things. This is what Jesus meant when he said: "No servant can serve two masters . . . Ye cannot serve God and mammon." (*Luke* 16:13).

With this, Jesus was not calling on us to fly from reality. What he clearly meant and in fact carried out in his own life was this: we certainly can and should work in the world with all our capability and with all the means which are given to us. We must master material things in the most practical way possible—but we must not let ourselves be mastered by them. We must not become totally wrapped up in them or see them as the aim of our lives. *To serve*—which means to give our total allegiance, to give our undivided attention, to strive with all our might, to be completely given over and to see as our only aim in life—is something that we can and must do only with reference to the eternal Godhead in ourselves and in all things with which we are concerned.

Once again, Jesus formulated this principle in the simplest and clearest way: "But seek ye first the kingdom of God (the wholeness of God) and his righteousness (lawfulness); and all these things shall be added unto you." (*Matthew* 6:33). That this is a rule which applies to all human actions in general, as well as constituting the most effective health rule for body, mind and soul in the spirit—this is something which can be confirmed by anyone who has once started to live according to its precepts.

In the mountains, outside the caves, we heal the local people who come from far and wide. Josephine Sison operates on them. Province of Quirino on the Philippines, 1982

Report by Dr. med. Hans Nägeli, Zurich

Psychic Surgery and Spiritual Healing

Logurgy and spiritual healing are based on common theoretical premises. In both methods of therapy, we discern a *psycho-potential* of energy waves which are still today difficult to measure and which come to the healer from cosmic sources.

To describe logurgy as psycho-surgery or para-surgery is correct only in cases where an immediately visible intervention in the body takes place. Until now, I know of only two logurgy operators who cut the skin to a depth of admittedly only about two millimetres and caused an opening—which in the case of only one of these healers closed up again immediately after the treatment but left a visible scar. Such an event can be described as psycho-surgery, even though during the operation the hand does not touch the body. In my opinion, the cut is caused by concentrated imagination, in the course of which the healer—usually in a psychic state of trance—imagines with great intensity the opening up of the skin. While doing this, he imitates a cutting motion with his index finger about 20 centimetres above the place which is to be opened up. But in fact the hand which leaves its effect on the body and appears to penetrate it represents a symbol rather than an instrument. Indeed, in many cases, and particularly with spiritual healers in the West, the hand is the bearer of ethereal energy waves which issue from the palm and the tips of the fingers. The meridian points of issue on both the fingertips and the palms of the hand are known to us from acupuncture.

One of the most frequent objections to spiritual healing, and above all to logurgy, is met in the statement that these phenomena contradict scientific thinking and proven experience. Penetration of a finger or even of an entire hand into a living body—the event which I have just described was an exceptional case—without the edge of a wound being visible or without the displacement of tissue is considered a thing of impossibility. But there do exist very rare plants which only a few botanists ever have the chance to see. To deny their existence would be as short-sighted as the denial of logurgy by representatives of the natural sciences who have never come across the phenomenon. Many people know nothing whatever about this kind of treatment or know about it only through films or in an unfavourable light through prejudiced "research journeys". There exist evil-intentioned, deliberate falsehoods which are spread through the media by successful pseudo-scientists. It happens that in their particular branch certain "very talented" researchers often make astonishing "observations". Thus, a certain university professor, who is a recognised expert on hypnosis, has stated that patients are hypnotised by logurgy operators and that their successes are of a purely suggestive nature. Yet it is possible to learn from every person treated that they remained wide awake during the whole occurrence and that they were able to observe every phase of treatment in exactly the same way as those standing about them.

A prejudiced person who clings only to what is known, by which he means the dominating scientific opinion of the time, hinders free research, particularly the kind which was postulated by the Anglo-German natural scientist, William Herschel (1738-1822), who wrote: "The complete observer will keep his eyes open in all the parts of knowledge, so that he can take into account every event which, according to generally accepted theories ought *not* to occur, for precisely *these are the facts which lead to new discoveries." In this sense, the possibilities of interpretation which lead to an intellectual opening to logurgy and healing by the spirit have long been available. But this has not been within the natural sciences* which are committed to material things and causality, but within *natural philosophy* which is to be understood as research into nature and meaning. In his comparison of both these academic directions, the well-known physiologist, Professor W. Blasius from Giessen, emphasised that *both* of them should be described as sciences. W. Heitler, the recently deceased teacher of theoretical physics at Zurich University, wrote in his book *Man and Scientific Knowledge* (Vieweg, Volume 116): "The atom is no longer even conceivable in space and time. Alone to describe it, profound mathematical concepts are necessary. So the atom can hardly be understood as a purely material thing. This means that even physics, and in particularly strong measure atomic physics, brings up metaphysical questions." Metaphysical realities are those which are outside time and space. In the cases of spiritual healing and logurgical interventions in the body, this is precisely the case: it is not exclusively a matter of relationships in space but of relationships in a given state of affairs. The state of matter is changed. On the basis of our experience with water, we know quite a lot about the transformation of a given state of matter from the solid state to the liquid state and to the formation of steam. But that an object can be transformed from a solid state into an invisible and impalpable state and vice versa, as indeed happens in occurrences like dematerialisation and rematerialisation, is not as yet susceptible to explanation. Around the turn of the century—and today this seems to be still the case only in England and Brazil—spirits materialised in such completeness during spiritualist seances that the pulse-rate could be checked by university professors, and even the warmth of the body could be felt. Soon after, these beings dissolved once more into the ethereal—which means that they returned to the energy form which they possessed before the seance. Recognised thinkers of that time, such as Sir William Crookes, Gustave Geley etc, were witnesses to this.

Anyone who follows parapsychological literature carefully will discover that within the human sphere there are very many circumstances in which objects can materialise and dematerialise. I myself have not only experienced this many times in my own life, but I have also heard about it in reports by reliable witnesses. So for me personally there is no longer any room for doubt. That these facts remain practically unknown is due to the dogmatic limitations of many cultivated people who always put matter above spirit. The result is that such events are not taken seriously *a priori* and are condemned as deceptions. That this is no longer in accordance with modern research in physics has already been mentioned. I have tried in my books (H. Nägeli-Osjord: *Logurgy in the Philippines*, Otto Reichl Verlag, Second Edition, 1982; H. Nägeli-Osjord: *Possession and Exorcism*, Otto Richl Verlag, 1983) to demonstrate such matters, above all the phenomenon of psycho-plastics. As an expert in paranormal phenomena, I have received a host of patients from surrounding European countries, and naturally above all from Switzerland, who have given me a view of this area of knowledge which is probably bettered by no university professor and no psychiatrist. So if I say that in all these cases not perhaps an identical but a similar pattern of behaviour has been observed, then the probability of its genuineness grows very considerably. In these remarks, I am thinking particularly of the phenomenon of possession in its very varied forms. Particularly in cases of those possessed by spirits, we meet a large number of materialisations and dematerialisations, such as psycho-plastics, and distortion of matter, through the work of spirits. Disease symptoms connected with possession and obsession are ignored in university clinics and are misdiagnosed as schizophrenia, hysteria and epilepsy, although the patient in no way fits the normal characteristics of the disease named. For natural scientists, spiritual life is automatically extinguished at the same time as the material decay of the body. Spiritual life of any kind is unthinkable in their book.

The fact that materialisation, dematerialisation and psycho-plastics represent realities—something that the next generation will perhaps no longer cast doubt upon—is of the highest importance for spiritual healing.

How, then, does spiritual healing work? Here we must refer to the spiritual bodies, or, rather, the ethereal bodies, the "subtle bodies" of Paracelsus. In all the great cultures of the ancient world, amongst all non-intellectualised people still today, in the whole of Eastern thought, the subtle body represents an undisputed truth. It is the Egyption "Ka", the Greek *soma pneumatikon* and the Chinese "shenli", to name just these three. Our materialist-rationalist thought of today has left the subtle body completely out of account because it is a quantity which cannot be measured or scientifically proved. But Indian thought, as described in *Tantra Vidya*, actually counts thought at the mental level (Buddhi) and feeling at the astral level (Manas) as part of matter. An even greater concentration is represented by the ethereal level (Prana), the central creative force in the anthroposophical way of thinking. This is the placenta strata of all bodies in process of formation, as well as of the material body itself. These are whole spheres of thought which for us are described as psychic or spiritual but in Indian teaching represent material things. "Since all spheres, from the mental to the substantial, form a living continuum, any material transformations amongst them are possible in principle." (O. M. Hinze. *Tantra Vidya*, second edition, pages 225 ff.). This means that an intensive thought (the mental sphere), particularly in cases of strong emotional involvement (the astral sphere), can be transformed in the sense of an increase in concentration into a material form which corresponds to the intellectual idea. Whoever has experienced Satya Sai Baba in Bangalore and Sri Ganapthy Sachchidananda in Mysore (South India) is aware of the numerous materialisations which these two Indian avatars bring about every day. This is not illusion. Materialisations and psycho-plastics, or transformations, can only happen within the bounds of a profound religious conviction, which presupposes help from the existence and power of God. These things provide invisible forces which help to transform ethereal into substantial forms. In simple but inner prayers to hour-long rituals, God's healing favour is called down. We also find this phenomenon with all the significant spiritual healers of Europe.

Sai Baba (Howet Murphet: *Sai Baba*, Fischer-Tagebuch 1978, p. 191) is supposed to have transformed a lump of granite into a statue of a flute-playing Krishna by simply blowing upon it. This can be seen first as transformation, or psycho-plastics, and then also as transmutation, as the hard granite changes into the sweetness of Krishna. This was achieved by Sai Baba on an impulse, in order to bring material light to a philosophical question. He wanted to make it understood that beyond all molecules God reigns and that with his spiritual power he is capable of achieving any transformation of matter.

Knowledge about the existence of an ethereal body, which as matter in the Tantric sense is capable of all material transformations, and the experience that thoughts and imaginary powers, or ethereal energy, are capable of changing not only so-called dead matter (see Uri Geller, among others) but can also change the subtle body of the human organism, must bring about understanding of the occurrences on which logurgy and all spiritual healing are based. In the practice of logurgy in the Philippines and in other countries where individuals at simple levels of the population are not yet intellectualised and where a high mediumistic talent has not thereby been forfeited, there very often occur much more spectacular events than we can ever see in the sphere of spiritual healing in the Western world. The fact that people who are not intellectualised have a much greater sensitivity to the *nature* of things and to religious realities makes possibile direct and immediate cures. This explains the dematerialisation of surrounding body tissue which allows the hand of the healer to remove tumours and all manner of suppurative centres directly from within the body. This also makes it easier to understand the appearance of foreign objects from within the body as materialisations. But beyond this the energy produced by healing waves from the hands and fingers plays the same role as with our spiritual healers. The basic principles behind all these kinds of healing are the same.

At this point, I would like to state with every possible emphasis that all spiritual healing reaches the subtle body of the sick person as an ethereal emanation, whether it comes directly from the hand or, in the case of healing from a distance, from the ethereal centres of the brain. When the subtle body is harmonised, then all the parts of the organic body will be harmonised—for every organ has its own ethereal equivalent. With very strong healers, this may happen immediately, but in most cases the transformation requires a certain length of time, sometimes even months. Such a delay often sheds positive light on an event which may have been brought forward as evidence of fraud in spiritual healing. For example, it is not rare for logurgy operators in the Philippines to materialise gallstones and hand them over to the patient. But in later analysis these prove to be simply pebbles. These fit in with the concept of the healer, but not with our physiological ideas. An X-ray picture taken immediately after the return of the patient from the healer will indicate that the stones remain in the gallbladder. In very many cases, however, the attacks of pain will cease immediately after the intervention of the healer and in one to two months the stones will be seen to have dissolved naturally. This was the final effect of the harmonised subtle body of the gall-bladder. It is more than understandable that all this might appear to a conventional doctor as pure deception, combined perhaps with the power of positive suggestion. Within today's philosophy of medicine, there is indeed no other possible solution. As long as the existence of an ethereal body is not recognized, an event of this kind remains entirely alien to nature and is therefore unbelievable. We may remember in this connection the words of Paracelsus, the doctor of medieval days who today has come back into high consideration and honour: "If a doctor knows no more of the subtle body than he knows about the organic body, then he is no doctor." As I have already said, Paracelsus was until only a few decades ago rejected as a confused mind, while today he is recognised as a genius and the renovator of the medicine of the Middle Ages. It needed only one more step for full spiritual comprehension of his main idea, the close link between the subtle body and the organic body. If this step had been taken, orthodox medicine would have emerged from its long surpassed dogmatic attitude of material causal thinking, in exactly the same way as modern physics have been seen to cast off outdated attitudes. This would have made it possible to put the spiritual powers of individuals as healing factors on the same level as chemical and technical factors. It would also have been possible to estimate which was most needed in individual cases, and the co-operation of conventional medicine and the natural healing arts would have been established. This has to a large degree already been achieved in England. Continental Europe will certainly follow this model.

To summarise, it should be emphasised that with logurgy and with every kind of spiritual healing two spheres of action exist and both of them can be precisely observed:

1. The influence and the concentration of thought impulses from the mental and astral layers of the healer on the subtle body of the patient. This is an ethereal transformation, in the sense of the *Tantra Vidya*, a harmonising form of psycho-plastics, which transfers itself in concentrated form from the subtle body to the organic body, in the same way as the ethereal body reflects the physical body.

2. Ethereal, positive-cosmic energies are gathered together in the Chakra stream through the meridians of the healer into the energy potential of the patient and harmonise—as in the Yin-Yang polarity in acupuncture—certain parts of the body, so that here also the ethereal body is brought into balance *in a primary phase*. In the secondary phase, this is communicated to the diseased organ.

Ecumenical service in the Catholic Church at Wald in Switzerland, with healing meditation led by Madeleine. (Participants: the Catholic priest, A. Ambauen, the Protestant priest and qualified psychologist, Guenther Schumacher). 19th August, 1984.

The first way is certainly the most demanding. But both possibilities can be combined according to the capacities of the healer.

In spiritual healing in the West, we find mostly the second way. Sometimes this will be felt to be the best and the most holy since it is untouched by the—in most cases subconscious—effects of the human will. God and his cosmic influence—or his positive representatives, the numinous spirits—are the only sources of power. The fact that this is so needs no human decision. Throughout spiritual healing, we recognise the reign of the Godhead.

PAUL ERNST, NOTARY PUBLIC
LENZBURG

5000 Lenzburg, 9th April 1985

Notarial Attestation

The undersigned, Paul Ernst, Notary Public in the Canton of Aargau, Switzerland, whose offices are in Lenzburg, hereby confirms that the letters of acknowledgement printed in Chapter IV of this book correspond to the originals. Some of these letters have been abridged and their style and spelling corrected where necessary but no changes have been made in their sense. I can therefore certify that the letters of acknowledgement here reproduced are true to the originals.

Lenzburg, 9th April 1985

The Notary Public
signed: Paul Ernst

Seal of a Notary Public
of the Swiss Canton of
Aargau

IV. Letters of Acknowledgement

Examples of healing attested by patients.

For reasons of discretion the family and place names have not been indicated in full. All the letters of acknowledgement have been conscientiously examined by our Lenzburg Notary Public, Paul Ernst (see previous page).

Muscular Atrophy

About thirty years ago my brother contracted a serious, incurable disease very little known in Switzerland. Miosotis, a type of muscular astrophy. He visited well-known doctors but with no success. A relative who was then chief medical officer at Muri District Hospital took him along to a medical congress, after which we were given the devastating news that there was no hope for the twenty-eight-year-old man. My brother had a magnificent farm and a happy young family. Naturopaths were also unable to help. Only prayer remained. A priest from the Capucine monastery in Sursee visited us during that difficult time on his collecting round, as was his annual custom. When he saw my brother, who already bore the stamp of approaching death, he suggested that we take him to Mr. Michel in Lenzburg. Even if it all seemed beyond hope, we nevertheless set out immediately. Mr. Michel welcomed us with a fatherly smile. "It is literally the last minute but with God's blessing and a bit of luck things ought to improve," he said. We were filled with fresh hope and great confidence after the first treatment. This was followed by many more. For us it was—and still is—a miracle that this terrible disease was vanquished by Mr. Hermann Michel and, later, by his daughter, Madeleine Riedel-Michel. My brother has enjoyed excellent health since that time. My thanks go beyond the grave to Mr. Michel. And our grateful recognition is also due to Mrs. Riedel.

(Author's remark: *God did the work; we were only His instruments.*)

Hernia of an Intervertebral Disc/Paralysis

In 1952 I suffered from dreadful pain in my lower back (hernia of an intervertebral disc) and could hardly walk. I went to Mr. Michel in Heiden for a course of treatment, twice a day. Ten days later I returned home free from pain.

In 1948 my sixty-eight-year-old mother had to have a kidney operation and during the days that followed my mother suffered no pain and was cured by Mr. Michel's support.

My left foot was paralyzed as the result of a surgical error during an operation for varicose veins. I was taken twice weekly to Mrs. Riedel for treatment. Nine weeks later I was able once more to stand and a little later also to walk. I owe Mrs. Riedel a tremendous debt of gratitude.

Serious General Health Crisis

I first met your father thirty-three years ago. At that time he helped me over a serious general health crisis. When I asked him what we should do if the crisis recurred in the years ahead, he answered quite simply, "Well, we'll just take it away again." For twenty years, until he died, he gave very considerable support to the orphanage and home for children and young people with behavioural problems which I ran. Thanks to his and, in subsequent years, your own tremendous support we have been able to offer many children security and bring them up to be valid citizens. I am grateful to both you and your father that I was allowed to help. The crisis mentioned above recurred thirty years later and I did not know what to do since your father had just died. During a critical night I called your father in my mind and asked for his help. On that very day you came to visit us once more after an interval of several years. You asked quite spontaneously what was wrong here—you had had an inner conviction that you were needed here. And you set about treating me at once. Subsequently I visited your practice once a week.

For three years you gave me the strength to do what I had to do for those who needed me. You helped me and I passed that help on to others. During these three years you have enabled me to become more and more "detached" and have helped me to increased inner vision. For me this is the most precious gift since the increase in inner vision enabled me to help more intensively. And what is more worthwhile than to help a suffering child or young person or adult? All the pain I had to bear has not been in vain and I thank God that he allowed me to take this path. He permitted the pain but at just the right moment he sent me a helper—first your father, then you.

Mr. R. in B.

Neurodystonia/Cyanosis (blue asphyxia)

The first visit to Lenzburg was, in a manner of speaking, my wife's last chance to regain health. She suffered from severe neurodystonia and the doctors were unable to help her apart from giving her pills and injections. As long as I live I shall not forget that first treatment, given at the time by your father who unhappily died far too young.

On our way home my wife said she would like something to eat as soon as possible—dumplings, of all things. She got her dumplings and I was overjoyed, after so many months, to see her in a positive frame of mind and enjoying life again. Many sessions of treatment followed and she continued to improve. In the meantime we had discovered that you were able to cure all manner of ailments and, consequently, our whole family benefited from your healing gifts.

I should like to describe the particularly striking case of our new-born granddaughter. An hour after the child was born the nurse luckily noticed that Barbara was having difficulty with her breathing; she was already blue in the face. She was promptly transferred to the intensive care unit of the childrens's hospital where she was given oxygen. We telephoned our alarm to you and Barbara received immediate help. The doctors were amazed that the dreadful crisis passed so quickly.

In the meantime we have appealed to you for help on several occasions and your teletherapy has always helped. After each treatment my wife and I feel as if our batteries had been recharged while, at the same time, an inner peace and happiness has been restored. In our home you have long since ceased to be "Mrs. Riedel", having become "our Madeleine".

Mr. and Mrs. S. in B.

Depression

By nature I am a happy, mostly positive person. About sixteen years ago, when I was forty-three, a problem that had been worrying me for months caused my legs to give way. I viewed everything negatively and wanted only to die; I was often tempted to throw myself under a passing car. I had a good husband and four children, the youngest of whom was only three. I suffered from insomnia so the doctor prescribed antidepressants and sleeping pills. Although this made things more bearable I was benumbed for a whole year.

One day I knelt down in my bedroom and asked God to show me the way since the whole family was suffering dreadfully because of my condition. Later, in the living room, I turned on the radio. The first sentence I heard was, "My patients suffer from nervous disorders." I pricked up my ears. The man speaking was Mr. Michel in Lenzburg, Mrs. Riedel's father. Some of his patients spoke as well.

Suddenly I knew that my prayer had been answered. The first time I went to Lenzburg Mr. Michel assured me that he and Mrs. Riedel, who worked with him, could help me. He said I should be patient since anything that had been dammed up for months could not just be made to vanish.

After a period of regular treatment I became gradually calmer. The medicines were slowly reduced until I ceased taking them altogether. I recovered and was deeply grateful to Mr. Hermann Michel and Mrs. Riedel for the gift of renewed health. Above all, I thanked God who had heard my prayer and shown me the way.

For sixteen years everything went well and then I had another attack as the result of a harsh blow dealt by fate. I went straight to Mrs. Riedel. This time I took part in the healing meditation sessions at the week-end before each treatment and I tried hard to think positively. I thank God that I again recovered and that there are people like these to help me along the way.

Mrs. B. in Z.

Cerebral Cramp (teletherapy)

My son and daughter often had severe cerebral cramp. The first time my son had one of these attacks I telephoned Mr. Michel and asked him

to help. He said he would intervene immediately. The next day I asked
Mr. Michel what had been wrong and he told me that if I had waited
until this morning before telephoning my son would no long have been
alive.

Our family has had to bear a great deal of adversity but Mr. Michel
and Mrs. Riedel have always been able to fend off the worst.
Throughout all these disturbances, such as circulatory malfunctions,
urinary troubles, nerve cramps, peritonitis and even kidney stones,
Mrs. Riedel has always been able to relieve the pain through
teletherapy.

The L. family in W.

A patient once dedicated this poem to me. I have become very fond of
it and should like to share it with my readers:

HEALING HANDS

Hands given and blessed by God,
Tireless hands that heal and strengthen,
Hands that evil turn to good.
God preserve these hands, these gifts
That rid the soul of fear and ill—
This noble sense that so uplifts.
Happy the child who, thus endowed, is called by a vocation.
Protect, O God, these hands that heal and strengthen in privation.

Burns

During an accident on 25th October, 1983, I suffered first and
second degree burns which affected my whole face, neck, chest,
abdomen and parts of my arms and legs.

Mrs. Madeleine Riedel learned of these burns about four hours after
the accident and treated me immediately—with great success.

The doctor wanted to keep me in hospital for three weeks so that the
burns could heal but, to the surprise of all the medical staff, I was able
to go home after ten days.

My thanks go to Mrs. Riedel for her work which was wellnigh
miraculous. I have suffered no after-effects whatever from the burns.

Mr. H. in S.

Kidney Operation

It was an astounding fact but, each time you treated me for extremely painful attacks of renal colic, the pain disappeared.

After the operation, which you advised me to have, I had great difficulty recovering. I returned to you and felt better after each treatment. My physical condition had also taken its toll on my nerves. Above all I suffered from uncontrollable muscular spasms in my right arm which blocked both middle fingers so that I was unable to type. This worried me as I feared I should no longer be able to continue my work as a secretary. The doctors could offer no help. But here, too, you helped me, Mrs. Riedel. Later on I had an acne-like rash on my face with fever blisters. The family doctor prescribed antibiotics which prevented the rash from spreading but did not heal it. You treated me twice and the rash gradually lessened and was finally completely cured.

Words cannot express what your help meant to me.

Mrs. W. in Z.

Preparation for a Prostate Operation and Post-Operative Care

Last November I was forced to undergo a prostate operation—no small matter at seventy-six. Mrs. Riedel already gave me one individual treatment before the operation to enable me to gather the necessary strength for the difficult time ahead. After the operation, while I was in the intensive care unit, Mrs. Riedel gave me teletherapy.

After four weeks in hospital I went to Mrs. Riedel for a second session of individual treatment. My recovery progressed rapidly.

During the third week after leaving hospital I was treated a third time and I was then already able not only to take quite long walks with my wife and our dog but also to drive my car again. Friends and neighbours were astonished at my rapid recovery.

I am convinced that it was only Mrs. Riedel's kind help, which served to complement the medical treatment, that made this possible.

Mrs. S. in W.

Paralysis and Radiation Syndrome
Partial paralysis of the leg, Radiation myelopathy (following Hodgkin's disease, Stage 2)

I was paralyzed and confined to a wheelchair when my family doctor and I happened to go to the same lecture. This was how I met Mrs. Madeleine Riedel. I felt "at home" after a very short time, doubtless because of her exceptional magnetism.

She talked about her experiences with the spiritual healers in the Philippines and showed a great many slides. I learned about her being paralyzed as a child—and listened even more carefully.

My case history began with Hodgkin's disease (lymph gland tumour). Some of the metastases were surgically removed, the remainder, the main source in the heart and lung region, had to be treated by cobalt radiation.

This therapy caused the tumour to disappear but unfortunately also paralyzed everything below the radiation level and I was condemned to life in a wheelchair. A further price to be paid for removal of the tumour was great difficulty in breathing and pain in the region of the heart.

On top of all this there was the dreadful uncertainty as to whether I should live or soon die; this required untold strength on the part of a sick mother with two lively boys, one at kindergarten and the other in his first year at school. Friends and acquaintances told me about many other therapies which I tried and which also helped—foot reflexology, electro-acupuncture, insulation of the house against earth radiation, homeopathy, the application of cabbage leaves, black molasses (which, in the early days of my paralysis, immediately cured the pain in my back), magnetotherapy, courses of kefir and beetroot juice (which the oncological laboratory tests proved had given me sufficient blood) and, finally, spiritual healing. In addition to these therapies the family doctor prescribed physiotherapy and massage. Many kind people helped with nursing and housework. Relatives, friends and the women in the village encouraged me when things got difficult. All this sympathy had a healing effect on my soul just like every honest, loving, heartfelt word.

I was particularly impressed by the unknown eight-year-old boy that I met in Mrs. Madeleine Riedel's waiting-room who told his mother the following day that he wanted nothing for his birthday or for

Christmas—all he wished, he said, was that that paralyzed lady should be able to walk again!

Before I asked Mrs. Riedel for her unusual help I sought strength and a relief from my great pain from a magneto-therapist who, while he was treating me, felt in his own body much of the pain in my paralyzed legs and abdomen. This also always corresponded to the reflex zones in my feet, the meridians for the appropriate organs in my body, to the irido-diagnosis and the pressure points in my ears, all of which tell the truth.

I greatly enjoyed swimming in therapeutic waters or in the nearby Lake of Constance—for the first time in eight years. There I was finally able to breathe easily and even to swim on my back (I still have to learn breast-stroke and I shall be able to do that only when my back improves and I have the strength to hold up my head). Water does in all truth bear one up!

In addition to all these therapies I need a great deal of help from my husband (who has had to adapt himself in so many ways) and from the children who, in the meantime, have become big boys. Every day they see how much effort the smallest action demands of a paralyzed person—and so many are unfortunately impossible: washing and dressing oneself, turning round and turning over and sitting up in bed, fetching a book from the bookcase, going to the bathroom, going out of the house, propelling oneself along in a wheelchair (due to lack of strength) and so on.

These visible disabilities are more easily comprehended by the healthy than the psychic burden of the tremendous uncertainty involved—the question of length of life. In times such as this one grabs at every straw and warms oneself at every spark of hope. The blessing of sympathy alone is a great help in bearing the tortures of disability, Mrs. Madeleine Riedel, who sees herself as an instrument of God, came as such a spark into my life. She explained clearly to us, seekers after help that we all were, the importance of forgiving all those who do or have done us any wrong. Thus, deep in my heart, I had to forgive the doctor who had prescribed the excess of radiation that had led to my paralysis.

In recent times one reads in the Press that improved apparatus is now available. God be thanked that no more patients need suffer the agonies of such invalidism. God also be thanked that I met Madeleine Riedel, thus coming into contact with spiritual healing. This has helped me gradually to improve and to face life with a positive attitude.

The doctor is at present injecting a new medicine into the scarred tissue and this supports my hope for further improvement.

Thus, many people—doctors, therapists and healers—all work for the welfare of the patient. Direct co-operation among these helpers would be desirable.

Mrs. B. in S.

Childlessness

I have two children, both of whom I owe entirely to your healing powers. When children showed no sign of appearing and all the necessary medical examinations had been made, the only thing left to be done was a clearing of the Fallopian tubes. Since these were blocked by adhesions, this did not help and I was told that I must expect to remain childless.

In desperation I came to you and, after three months of regular treatment, I became pregnant!

We wanted a second child but unfortunately I had two miscarriages. When I once more became pregnant and another miscarriage threatened I came to you again for regular individual treatment. Afterwards I had to stay in bed for a long time and was unable to come to your practice. So you helped me through teletherapy—neither the doctor nor I believed the child could be born. The "Pap" test proved positive when I was three months pregnant, I had two myoma, an ovarian cyst and extensive adhesions. In spite of all this I give birth to a healthy daughter! I shall always be grateful for your tremendous help.

Our first child was always delicate and when he was 18-months-old it was found that he had too many white blood corpuscles and the blood picture and the lymphatic glands showed signs of leukaemia. He had to go straight to hospital for a bone-marrow puncture. I asked you to treat him by teletherapy and the blood test was already much improved the following day so that the doctors decided against the puncture. After several sessions of individual treatment with you his blood was once more in order. Neither we nor the doctors know precisely what was wrong. But we do know that you helped our child a great deal. Spiritual healing as a complement to medicine spared him unknown suffering.

Mrs. G. in U.

Disturbance of Growth and Metabolism

We should like to express our heartfelt thanks for helping our daughter slowly but surely to recover when she was suffering from metabolistic malfunctions and, consequently, disturbances of growth. For four years she has been privileged to benefit from your healing powers and the physical and spiritual progress she has made during this time is astonishing.   The S. Family in B.

Lung Tumour

I am a young girl and was taken to the doctor with a very bad cough and great difficulty in breathing. The doctors diagnosed a malignant tumour of the lung and I came to you for treatment. You helped me, Mrs. Riedel, to change my pessimism into optimism. You helped alleviate my cough and you prepared me so well for the surgery that nevertheless proved necessary that I got over the serious operation very well.

Even the severe pain in my back which followed the operation disappeared each time I visited you. I shall continue to come to you for treatment and to be strengthened by your healing hands. Thank you for all the good that you have done me.   Miss B. in D.

Retina

I am sixty-two, an accountant by profession and have worn reading glasses for about twenty years. Two years ago my sight worsened so rapidly that I was able to work only with the help of a fourfold magnifying glass. I went to see a local eye specialist and, later, I visited the eye clinic in Lausanne where I was told that my case was hopeless—indeed, that my condition would even worsen. Like all my father's relatives, I was suffering from premature, irrevocable aging of the retina. I should not completely lose my sight, they said, but it would constantly diminish. The hospital in Lausanne advised me to go to the Swiss disability insurance authorities, to give up my accountancy activities and to get myself recycled into another profession that would at least strain my eyes less.

Through a coincidence an acquaintance had advised me to go to Mrs. Madeleine Riedel in Lenzburg before taking official steps. I went to see her and during that first visit she told me that it would be possible to improve my condition but that it would cost me a great deal of patience. Although, in view of the diagnosis in Lausanne, I was very sceptical, after several visits to Mrs. Riedel I was miraculously able to continue my work without the help of a magnifying glass.

Today I feel as I did six years ago. I am 100% able to work, I can drive without much trouble and I can even indulge my hobby, doing crossword puzzles.

A thousand thanks to Mrs. Madeline Riedel who has been a fairy godmother to me.   Mr. J. in Y.

Asthma

There are not enough words to describe your healing powers! In November, 1982, Mrs. Madeleine Riedel treated me for the first time. I lay at home in bed with a very swollen face and my scalp hurt quite dreadfully.

My doctor took no further steps since I suffer from asthma. A good friend made an appointment for me to see Mrs. Riedel—I was lucky and very soon I was in her consulting room. The treatment was most effective and relieved me a great deal. Afterwards I wept most bitterly and deep sobs racked my whole body for a long time. After the hour's journey home my face was normal again.

It was almost unbelievable and friends and acquaintances came to my home to see this miracle. I had confidence in Mrs. Riedel and continued with the treatment.

In February, 1983, I was taken seriously ill with asthma and my heart started giving trouble as well—I had had this kind of difficulty for ten years. When I stood in this state beside Mrs. Riedel it was as if I had been struck by lightning. The treatment on that occasion was very trying. That night I had to be taken to the intensive care unit at our local hospital where I remained unconscious for fifteen hours. Since that night the dreadful attacks have never recurred. I can once more move quite normally.

Mrs. Riedel's power has given me new life. I go to her twice a month for treatment and hope I may continue to do so.   Mrs. M. in W.

Author's note: this patient's fifteen-hour loss of consciousness is a very rare but very healing reaction by virtue of which she was given a new life.

Diagnosis—Blindness

Before you fly off to the Philippines I very particularly want to thank you once again most sincerely for all the good that you do daily to so many people but especially for the wonder that you have wrought in me.

When I came to you many years ago I was a totally broken woman, incapable of living with the diagnosis of blindness given me. By your faith you helped me not to give up but to fight on. After all those well-known specialists you were the first person to give me hope, the first person who did not just say I should have to learn to live with the findings.

Today my sight is better than ever; I need only very weak spectacles. I have a very exacting profession and enjoy my family and my life which I should otherwise doubtless have ended. The treatment has also brought great growth in my powers of awareness.

Mrs. F. in Z.

Eyes—Retinal Detachment

In Spring 1977 I noticed a serious change in the sight of my right eye. Mrs. Riedel advised me to see an eye specialist who diagnosed retinal detachment and advised against reattachment of the retina. Regular treatment from Mrs. Riedel, together with compresses using "Swedish Bitter Herbal Extract" (Schwedentropfen), the retina has reattached itself where it was torn off and, a year later, I can see much better. The situation has so improved that I am able to exercise my profession of foot specialist in spite of my seventy-four years. My general health is also constantly consolidated with my digestion, above all, being regulated and maintained on a good basis.

Mrs. J. in B.

Rheumatoid Arthritis

This woman wrote among other things:

My nephew's thirty-six-year-old wife suffered at intervals from rheumatoid arthritic pain in her jaw, shoulders, hips and legs. The doctors prescribed analgesics (painkillers) in packets of 100 tablets. There came a time when the patient no longer tolerated these and serious sceondary effects set in. Mrs. Riedel treated the patient seven times and healed her completely. In the six years that have passed since that time the pain has never recurred.

Mrs. J. in B.

Intestines

(This patient was healed in co-operation with a doctor of my acquaintance, Dr. F. in A.)

A few years ago I moved to a town where I had no friends or acquaintances and I felt very lost and unhappy. My long way to work in Zurich was an additional burden. Shortly afterwards I was unexpectedly taken ill with acute inflammation and ulceration of the colon which was not, however, immediately diagnosed. An acquaintance suggested that Mrs. Riedel could certainly help me. Mrs. Riedel immediately recognized the gravity of my condition. She invested all her energies and decided that I should go to hospital to be examined. I was kept there as an emergency case. It was not only the medical treatment that helped. A positive approach to life and correct nutrition are also important and Mrs. Riedel taught me these facts.

Mrs. B. in L.

Bell's Palsy (facial paralysis)

Many years ago, after a bad cold, I suddenly contracted Bell's palsy in the left side of my face. Thanks to careful medical treatment and effective medicines I gradually returned to normal. However, I was left with constant headaches, some worse than others. A neighbour who had been treated by you suggested I visit you. I already knew at the time that you had helped many people. And, truly, your blessed hands also helped me.

I very soon felt a considerable improvement. You are like the sun whose warm rays give new strength. I shall always be grateful to you.

Mr. R. in R.

Paralysis following a Road Accident

Just how significant a human life is each of us can assess only in terms of his own—and at best when there is no longer any hope of medical help.

My life was still important to me after twenty-five years' suffering caused by a road accident. When I first visited you I had difficulty in walking, was slightly paralyzed and in constant pain that was often beyond bearing. Today I know that it was divine authority that showed me the way to you, dear Mrs. Riedel.

Even if, at first, you were not exactly encouraging, saying that a long path of treatment lay ahead of us, something told me that you could help—all I had to do was believe this hard enough. After the first treatment I already knew that my instinct had not deceived me. Further treatment followed.

For the first time in twenty-five years I am free from pain. Through individual treatment and healing meditation you have helped me to "find my way back to myself" and words cannot express how successful you have been.

Mrs. S. in B.

Circular Bald Patches

I have been suffering from hair loss for a little over two years. At first little round, bald patches appeared which gradually got bigger; my abundant hair became generally thinner.

I visited various doctors but right from the start I was told not to expect very much help. I should have to resign myself to my fate. I tried everything that was suggested to me but without any lasting success. I shut myself up at home more and more as I was ashamed to be seen. I was very depressed and could no longer look at myself in the mirror. My condition became so bad that only a wig gave me sufficient courage to go out of doors. When I heard by chance of Mrs. Riedel's successes I decided to see if her help could supplement my own efforts. There were already signs of success after several sessions of individual treatment: the hair loss ceased and new hair began to grow on the bald patches.

It will take much time and patience to complete the cure but I am so happy with the results already achieved.

Mrs. Madeleine Riedel has also wrought a transformation in my entire life. Today I am much calmer, more balanced and satisfied. the entire burden that had wrought such havoc with my nerves in years past has been cast off. I look forward and am happy and content.

Mrs. S. in A.

Eczema on the Feet

(Beat sent me a letter in which he had drawn two little feet. He wrote—in Swiss dialect—"My feet are perfectly well, thank you!" Beat, 30th October, 1983.)

Thanks to your help Beat's feet have been free from eczema for a whole year. We are most grateful to be relieved of this burden after so many years.

Mrs. M. in B.

Kidney Dialysis

In the middle of June, 1980, I was taken to the Cantonal Hospital in Aarau as an emergency. I soon knew that, in spite of long-standing hope to the contrary, my ailing kidneys would not recover but that I should become permanently reliant on the dialyser.

When I was discharged from hospital I had to get used to going to the hospital twice a week for four hours of blood-washing. It was not easy.

Suicide was never far from my mind—the idea of suddenly being thus disabled was a terrible load on my mind and all the well-intentioned remarks about worse things happening at sea were not much comfort.

But with the help of my husband and my two sons I discovered a worthwhile alternative to merely giving up—a life worth living in spite of everything. It was at that time that Mrs. Ammann recommended that I go to you for treatment and after I had read a report on your healing powers in a Baden newspaper I did eventually come to you, albeit after some hesitation. I wanted to do something to improve my state of health.

In hospital I had been told that the damaged kidney tissue would never regenerate. The aim at the time was one day to find a kidney donor.

So, after my first visit to you, I came every week for treatment for a whole year. At the same time I had to go twice a week to Aarau for four hours' dialysis. At the end of May, 1981, that is a year after dialysis commenced, the doctor was able to reduce it to twice three hours and then even to twice two hours weekly. Only those who need dialysis will be able to understand what even the tiniest reduction in the duration of this treatment means to a patient!

At the beginning of November that same year Professor Blumberg told me that the blood values would for the time being permit of dialysis being reduced to one treatment a week. The experiment was successful. In February, 1982 the same doctor informed me that he would like to cease dialysis altogether on condition that I came to Aarau every week for a blood test, at least at first. Things went on developing positively. I started going for tests only every second week. The test intervals became increasingly longer until they reached two months. This is how things stand at present, in March, 1984, and the values that allow me to live without dialysis remain constant. My visits to you, Mrs. Riedel have been reduced to twice monthly. It is a marvellous feeling to be no longer reliant on a machine. The doctors talk about "interim remission" that could last for weeks, months or years. Actual healing in cases of kidney disease such as mine has so far never been known. A course of the disease such as I have experienced is, according to the specialists, very rare.

Personally I am convinced that a small miracle has been wrought in me in which the psychic factor has played a very important role. All the support I received—yours in particular, Mrs. Riedel—helped to strengthen me. After each treatment I took fresh heart and gladly followed your advice to lead a meaningful life and not to withdraw into my shell. Short journeys between the sessions with the dialyser took me to Ticino (in southern Switzerland), Vienna and Rome and my long journey to Moscow after I had become independent of the machine is still a very vivid memory. While I was away the knowledge that I was being included in your meditation was a tremendous source of confidence. At the back of my mind there is a certain anxiety about that "interim remission" and I often ask myself why precisely I should number among the fortunate few of my fellow sufferers who have escaped—and what is help, what is grace and what is one's own strength?

I hope and pray that the present situation may last a long time and that I may be permitted to maintain my contact with you since this means a great deal to me.

                                                        Mrs. M. in W.

Author's note: in this case self-healing and divine strength helped a great deal since the patient was destined to recover.

I should very much like to co-operate officially and for long periods with doctors in regard to patients requiring kidney dialysis.

Long-hoped-for Doctoral Thesis

I am going to try and finish my thesis this year. This will mark the end of lengthy studies and the commencement of a new phase in my life. During this time you have helped me in many ways and I should like to take this opportunity of thanking you, Mrs. Riedel, most sincerely. I should also like to mention in particular one aspect of this help for which I am so grateful.

When I came to you for the first time not quite ten years ago I was in the middle of a serious educational crisis. At that time I was at grammar school and quite unable to pass any sort of examination at all. In the end I was thrown out of the cantonal school. After a great deal of work, strength of will and help from you I got myself back on to this path. Thanks to your help I was calm during exams and able to "put myself across". I was sometimes overcome by a warming, inner quiet and confidence without feeling in the least leaden or numbed.

Today I am convinced that my good—and sometimes even very good—exam results are due to these circumstances.

Mr. S. in F.

Chronic Nettle-Rash

For twenty-five years I have suffered from chronic nettle-rash. During this time I have visited numerous dermatologists and spent a lot of time in hospital.

A friend gave me Mrs. Madeleine Riedel's address and I went to her without a great deal of conviction. After my third visit I already felt an improvement and after the fifth I was cured without ever having taken any form of medicine—something I had previously had to do daily.

I travel to Lenzburg regularly from the Strasbourg region, with a friend who suffers from psoriasis. Mrs. Riedel's wonderful healing hands have helped her as well—for the last two years her rash has decreased and sometimes even ceased.

Madame D. and Madame D. K. in K., France.

Backache and Speech Impediment

When I came to you for the first time about five years ago I was as low as I could probably get from every point of view. I had had agonizing backache for many months that tortured me day and night.

On top of this I had family problems which almost brought me to the brink of desperation in spite of the support given me by my dear husband.

Thus, one day, I sat in your waiting-room on the advice of a friend. To be frank, Mrs. Riedel, I hadn't much hope. But while you were treating me and your hands glided over my spine I had the strange feeling of a lock snapping home. I felt a comforting warmth right to the tips of my fingers. That night I slept deeply and quietly. For some days I was still expecting the pain but, wonder of wonders, it had disappeared—literally wiped away and *it never returned*. And the tremendous problems that I had carried around with me like a heavy rucksack receded to a distance after several sessions of treatment from you. I felt how you were transferring inner strength to me.

Two years ago, when I started suffering from disturbed sleep with attacks of fear and difficulty in getting my breath, your blessed hands were once again able to help.

Our grandchild had an impediment in his speech and suffered inhibitions as a result. Here, too, you were able to heal. Today we have a happy, cheerful child.

May God preserve your wonderful healing gifts.

Mrs. A. in D.

Arm/Shoulder Syndrome

I have suffered for many years from an arm/shoulder syndrome and it was only recently that the reason for my suffering was discovered in a hospital—torn ligaments in the shoulder area on both sides

The pain was torture. An operation might have been able to help but it involves a great risk. I told Mrs. Madeleine Riedel my tale of woe and went to her regularly once a week with great success.

I am now almost free from pain and, thanks to Mrs. Riedel's treatment, I feel quite well again.

Mr. O. in L.

Virus in the Brain

Twelve years ago I was taken seriously ill with a brain virus. I had severe headaches day and night and I was attacked by dizziness at the least physical effort and after every meal. Even when I was in bed at night everything around me seemed to spin. The worst of it all was the state of fear which would suddenly overwhelm me and against which I was absolutely powerless. These came during the day and frequently also at night. I had the feeling that I should run away. Sometimes I was close to screaming aloud, the burden was so great. I was unable to watch television and barely able to drive in a car—the least bump or effort was too much. In addition there were attacks of nervous weakness which left me shaking. I have never before or since suffered a sickness against which there was nothing I could do.

Apart from God, I owe my recovery to Mrs. Riedel alone. I was in a very critical condition when I first went to her. She told me this frankly, remarking that I had been fortunate not to have suffered some kind of paralysis as well. But she gave me the hope that she would be able to help me. I was unutterably grateful to hear this since I was at the end of my tether.

At first I went about three times a week to Mrs. Riedel for treatment and then less frequently. At the beginning, step by step, things began to improve. Since Mrs. Riedel told me that the whole business would take a long time and a great deal of patience, and that I still had some difficult weeks ahead of me, I battled on and hoped for improvement.

After three very difficult months, during which Mrs. Madeleine gave me a lot of spiritual strength in addition to the treatment—she was always there to help me—, I was over the worst and felt I had literally been given a new life. I had suffered unspeakably but had received wonderful help through Mrs. Riedel. I cannot find adequate words with which to thank her. I hope that God will bless her and her activities and grant her so much good fortune that she will always be able to draw the strength she needs for her selfless service to suffering humanity.

Mrs. D. in W.

Prolapse of an Intervertebral Disc

When I came to you about the bed-wetting of our youngest child, little did I know that I should soon be soliciting your help for myself.

You succeeded at that time after just a few treatments in "drying out" our child and the nappies have been put into storage.

A few months later I suffered a prolapsed intervertebral disc. Since I wished at all events to aviod an operation I had to lie flat as much as possible for several weeks. My only ventures out of doors were the journeys to Lenzburg for your treatment. They brought me to you on a stretcher.

Thanks to your treatment the cramps I suffered were gradually relieved and my back got stronger and stronger. This was a year ago.

In order to strengthen my spiritual and, thus, also my physical resistance I still come to you at certain intervals and I am happy to see that my own energy is beginning to flow once again.

For some time now I have been bringing my small son with me. He suffers from difficulties with his vision and with your healing power we are endeavouring to support an optical correction prescribed by the doctor treating him.

Mrs. W. in R.

Chronic Headaches

Your (the writer uses the "Du" form, i.e. the informal form of address) healing treatment has helped greatly and pointed the way for me in the course of the years. It is already several years ago that I came to you for the first time with constant tension pains in my right side. I awoke every morning with more or less severe headaches and generally felt sick. I also always felt tired and unstrung. At that time I wore thick-lensed glasses and an eye operation was being considered. After your treatment various things began to improve.

First of all I was able to stop wearing my glasses. Your treatment in conjunction with eye exercises had relieved the tension in my eyes. The headaches became fewer and fewer and in time the nausea of the early morning also disappeared. The same thing applied to the pains in my body. Simultaneously there was also healing of the spirit—after some time I was able once again to pray and found my way back to God.

For some time now I have been pursuing healing activities myself. You know, Madeleine dear, that you have played an important part in these developments. I should like to take this opportunity of thanking you once again for all your trouble, your conversation, your affection and sympathy.

Mrs. H. in B.

Preparation for an Operation

The removal of the metal/pin in my ankle went well and I am heartily grateful for your great help. I am convinced that it was thanks to this help that I got through the hospitalization calmly and with courage.

Mrs. H. in Z.

Healing of a Liver Malfunction

Two reasons brought me to you in the Summer of 1983. The first was my liver which had been troubling me from time to time since I had undergone butasolidon treatment and the second was curiosity to see how you worked and whether you could help me.

During my first visit to you my attention was drawn to your group meditation and I decided to take part in this. The way you run these sessions on the basis of Christian faith appealed to me greatly and I have participated regularly ever since in order to help both myself and the others and to benefit to the full from the subsequent treatment. After the first treatment my liver was considerably worse; then it started to improve and after about six weeks the trouble was completely cured. As a kind of secondary effect I was also cured of a bad habit. Since childhood I had to fight against nail-biting. I no longer feel the "need" to do this.

I should like to thank you most particularly for the pioneer work you are doing with this healing meditation. It is only to be hoped that the experience gained is broadcast and that theologians and medical people hear about it as well. Through this work you are contributing to giving people a better and more all-round picture of their own potential. The first step has been taken but there is much to be done before this knowledge can break through certain established dogmas.

Mr. P. in L.

Healing of Skin Cancer

I want to say how very grateful I am that you are there to help so many people. I am always impressed anew, when I participate in your sessions of healing meditation, by how lovingly and sympathetically you integrate each person present into your circle.

Looking back, the path to the healing of my skin cancer seems a short one. However, the five months it took, during which I had to bend my thoughts to support the healing, were sometimes very difficult.

I was advised to come to you and regularly took part in your sessions of healing meditation. I felt immediately that I was more relaxed and that an inner quiet set in. The wonderful prayers were heartfelt and went to the heart. I have never experienced this warmth in our church. Thus, I went home every Sunday with a sense of fulfilment and used passages of your meditation every day. I conscientiously followed your instructions to activate my own healing powers. My family were able to see how the red swellings decreased and the wounds began to heal. I also followed the doctor's instructions carefully and the wounds were tended and bandaged daily. However, after four months the pain when the bandages were changed became unbearable in spite of the circumstance that the wounds were four-fifths healed. I could not bear anyone to touch me and I became deeply depressed. The following Sunday I came to the healing meditation session in tears, accompanied by my husband. During meditation I became calmer and after your treatment I went home with renewed energy. You had given me the courage to carry on and I trembled in the face of your unshakeable faith in God.

I recognized that Christ is the same as He was 2000 years ago. I pulled myself together again with all the strength I had in me and the miracle happened. Two weeks later all the wounds were healed. The doctor was delighted and demanded all sorts of examinations and tests. When it was confirmed that all the values were normal everywhere I was discharged and told I was cured. That was three months ago and I now feel stronger than ever. Whenever I can I shall continue to participate in your Sunday healing meditation since I know very well that each one brings me new energy. May you continue these sessions of healing meditation when you return from the Philippines so that many more people may be blessed by your loving activities.

Mrs. E. in S.

Pancreatitis, Subsequent Gallstone Operation and Periarthritis

After a gall-bladder operation I found my way from Bienne to Mrs.

Riedel in Lenzburg. The doctors were at their wits' end since I had already undergone all manner of other operations and radiation. Thus, I began taking part in the healing meditation sessions with subsequent individual treatment by Mrs. Riedel. This was the first time that I—as a trained nurse!—had come face to face with healing meditation. So I just let myself be guided and learnt slowly to eliminate all my tensions and fears, finding the strength to "return to myself". I learnt to love my fellow men more dearly, to become aware that I am not the only pebble on the beach and to wish my fellow men well in their affairs and in their health. I also learnt to forgive all those who had done me any wrong. The sessions of healing meditation brought me harmony of body, soul and spirit, tranquillity and the renewal linked therewith of my inexhaustible strength.

After the third session of healing meditation the pain that had been with me for more than a year began to decrease and after the tenth treatment it had entirely disappeared! The repeated radiation I had undergone had also partially paralyzed my legs. Here, too, there was an improvement. I am deeply grateful to Mrs. Riedel who, as an instrument of God, channels His help to all of us who suffer.

Mrs. H. in B.

Healing of Rheumatoid Arthritis

When I came to you for the first time on 15th May, 1983, I was a very sick woman. I had primary chronic rheumatoid arthritis and could no longer walk properly. All my joints were thick and swollen and, in spite of the medicines I had to take, I suffered intolerable pain. When you told me during that first consultation that I was too young to have to suffer such an illness and that I might expect healing I was as yet unable to believe you.

My husband drove me from Germany to Switzerland to see you every Sunday. The whole family watched with great joy the change being wrought in me. I became more and more mobile and I learnt how to laugh again. Now, seven months later, my joints are almost back to normal. I can walk and even run again without pain. I have also been able to resume my housewifely duties. And all that, dear Mrs. Riedel, I owe to you.

Mrs. R. in R., Germany.

My Experience During Healing Meditation

Quietly I step through the portal of my self and allow myself to be lovingly encircled by my self. My self vibrates in love, strength and harmony. O wonderful, shining security—just to be—just to be carried along! Humility, I plead for humility. Then my self opens and everything starts vibrating towards and through the next YOU—to a YOU. Filled with awe I feel that we are YOU and YOU are US—everything is one, joined together in the flow of life—love. Saturated with this love I let it vibrate just where it is at present obstructed. If we were all to attempt to do this in our own place, we should become human wholes and this endless whole is salvation and we have—come home.

My most sincere thanks for your honest and commited leadership of a movement of peace and liberation.

Your tremendous personal investment is all the more meaningful because you practise what you preach. A living example was always the best teacher and signpost in our human seeking.

Mrs. B. in Z.

Chronic Earache and Sore Throat; Relief of Arthrosis

The fact that I have been cured of the earache and sore throats that had plagued me uninterruptedly for two years is like something out of a fairy-tale. I had been to various specialists and had been declared a hopeless case. I sometimes hardly recognize myself for in 1975 I had been classified as 50% disabled as a result of far-reaching arthrosis of the entire vertebral column. Now I am once more able to turn my head and rotate my arm. To my amazement my sight and my hearing have improved, a circumstance I can qualify only as a miracle. My only regret, especially in winter, is that I live so far away from you. Whenever necessary, I listen to your healing meditation cassette and transport myself to the soothing atmosphere of your home. The sound of your voice brings me a sense of total security. And at week-ends I join you in spirit in your sessions of healing meditation. This has become part of my life and helps me over the difficult times.

Mrs. L. in M., France

Unbearable Burning in the Feet

It is not easy to describe my two years of suffering. It was sheer hell! The burning sensation spread from my feet throughout my whole body (this happened mostly at night). I found no relief and even had to forego my long walks. How many doctors have I sought out and how many medicines have I tried—all in vain! I just got worse and worse.

I recall in particular one winter's day. I particularly wanted to go for a walk but suddenly I was unable to walk at all. My feet burnt like fire. I took of my shoes and went barefoot out into the snow which melted without leaving either water or steam behind. A well-known neurologist told me there was no hope of a cure. But I never gave up. I continued searching until I found Madeleine Riedel. Through the sessions of healing meditation and individual treatment I have become entirely well again. I am once again able to work, to walk without any sense of burning. And I feel full of gladness to be alive.

Mrs. O. in A.

I should like to thank Mrs. Riedel for the sessions of healing meditation I was permitted to experience. Even the neighbours have noticed the positive change I have undergone.

Mrs. N. in E.

Accident—Shattered Bones

Two years ago I had an accident during which my left hand was pretty well demolished. An acquaintance suggested I ask you, dear Mrs. Riedel, to treat me by teletherapy as long as I had to wear the plaster cast and subsequently to come to you for individual treatment. When the plaster was removed the hand and thumb joints that had been so shattered were entirely in order. Thanks to the teletherapy I suffered no pain either before or after removal of the cast in spite of the fact that the hand and thumb joints had been so seriously shattered. The first time I came to you for treatment, all heaviness left me as I entered your house and I felt indescribably light-hearted and at home. This feeling stayed with me during the session of healing meditation. Beside me sat a gentleman from the Philippines and I was permitted to experience this great strength, this warmth which flowed throug my body and made me completely calm.

My other ailments such as arthrosis of sixteen years' standing, a diaphragmatic hernia, damage to the vertebral column, a damaged auricular nerve and bad feet all gradually improved. I have had no more attacks of dizziness. The pain all disappeared and I was once more able to walk properly.

My son's headaches were also cured by several sessions of treatment.

Mrs. M. in L.

Depression

I came to you as a human wreck with severe depression after having been to various doctors during the previous year, none of whom were able to help me. I was no longer even able to add five and five, I was filled with unspeakable dread, complexes and feelings of inferiority. My brain was totally blocked and every thought required an enormous effort that was sheer torture. All my family wanted to do was send me to a mental home! One of my sisters-in-law even tried to awaken me from my apathy by slapping my face. It was then that I came to you, after having also contemplated suicide.

You gave me confidence and courage and the hope that I would recover. After some five or six sessions of individual treatment something suddenly went "click" and I was once again the self-assured, happy woman I had been before. After I had come to your lecture in Liestal—having already recovered—my blood pressure suddenly went up (220/120). I took part in the sessions of group meditation and within a short time my blood pressure had returned to normal.

You were also immediately able to heal an attack of sciatica.

Mrs. S. in P., Italy

Paralyzed Optic Nerve caused by a Minor Stroke

I was seriously affected by concussion accompanied by influenza and a subsequent slight stroke on the left side of my head, all consequent upon a fall on the ice. My eye constantly watered. Doctors and ophthalmologists were unable to help and I was forced to walk around with my eye covered like Mosche Dyan.

My daughter was being treated by Mrs. Riedel and she made an appointment for me too. I went three times a week for the first two weeks and after that twice a week for treatment and very soon my eye stopped watering and I was able to get rid of my dressing. Since then my eye has been in order.

The fall I had suffered had left me with attacks of depression. Happily Mrs. Riedel was also able to help me here. On Saturdays I go regularly to the sessions of healing meditation which give me a great deal of strength. In this way, at the age of eighty, I have been given a new lease of life.

Mr. K. in L.

Retching; Pain in Hips and Legs

It is with great pleasure that I can tell you of the success of your healing meditation and individual treatment.

My three ailments were retching and hip and leg pains, all of which you have cured with your wonderful healing hands.

Mrs. O. in Z.

Varicose Ulcers

I should like to thank you for your great help—I had varicose ulcers on both legs and suffered great pain. After coming to you three times for treatment the pain had already greatly decreased and after regular healing meditation and individual treatment for some time one leg is already completely cured.

Mrs. A. in A.

Neurodystonia

My body was greatly weakened since I suffered from neurodystonia and severe depression. I came to the sessions of healing meditation which did me a great deal of good as the strength present in the group is particularly marked. Each person present has something to give the others. We have urgent need of this method of healing for I have experienced in my own body and soul how wonderfully these forces can work.

Mrs. M. in N.

Tom Johanson at the International Healers' Congress in Baguio on the Philippines.

The Stress of an Important Examination (Medical Studies)

Sometimes it never rains but it pours! I had an important examination ahead of me, my mother was not well and I was beset by cares and problems. I began to notice that my energy was beginning to show signs of wear and tear. The result was disturbances of my sleep pattern, palpitations, difficulties in concentrating, disinclination to study and fatigue. However, I was determined to pass my exam.

I obtained Mrs. Riedel's address at a lecture on spiritual healing given by Mr. Rudolf Passian. After the first treatment I was already able to sleep better and I was no longer bothered by palpitations. This increased the nervous energy that sleep restores. Little by little my powers of concentration also improved and I had the feeling of being mentally fit in spite of all my studying. I now take part in the sessions of healing meditation regularly for they represent a source of energy for me. I get tired less easily and my endurance is gradually increasing so that I am much encouraged.

Miss O. in A.

Lack of Self-Confidence

Before I met Mrs. Riedel I was in bad shape. My nerves had reached breaking-point since I had been forced to declare bankruptcy. For this reason I had considerable debts. At the same time I was divorced from my wife. I saw no point in living at all and wanted to commit suicide.

For some time now I have been participating in the sessions of healing meditation with subsequent individual treatment and I feel a great deal better. I have gained self-confidence and I go home feeling strengthened. I should like to thank Mrs. Riedel for her great help.

Mr. S. in T.

New Optimism

Your treatment has helped me to find new courage to face life. Through healing meditation I have learnt that Christian love for one's neighbour is of great importance these days when all that counts is performance and profit. That hour all to myself and yet in good company gave me strength to cope with the entire week.

In our family profession and education count a great deal. Since I am not so successful as my brothers and sisters I always felt I was inferior.

Thanks to your treatment and the group sessions of healing meditation I have learnt that each individual is loved for himself alone and that there are far more important things in life than money and success. I have learnt to accept myself as I am.

Miss H. in L.

I should like to thank you from the bottom of my heart for the tremendous help and strength I was privileged to gain through you. My negative aproach to life and my sick soul have been completely changed in a positive and health-giving sense. I am so thankful that I was led to you. No matter how hard the path appears, with your help I shall reach my objective.

Mrs. K. in G.

I had the privilege of taking part in several of your sessions of healing meditation on Saturdays. They gave me so much strength that the path ahead of me is now clear and I am able to tread it alone. Thank you again most sincerely.

Mrs. L. in R.

It does one good to know that there are still people who offer their unstinting help to the suffering. I am delighted to be able to tell you that your sessions of healing meditation have brought me a good step closer to recovery. There is still a long way to go but my faith, like yours, is firm and I am assured that you will entirely cure me.

Mr. R. in E.

Consequences of an Accident

When our child lay badly injured in hospital and we were worried out of our wits, Madeleine Riedel, the healer, was brought to our attention. I told her about the injuries to our child and my own state of desperation. The healer was willing to include our child in her prayers, to treat him by teletherapy. Since then I have regularly taken part in the Sunday sessions of healing meditation with subsequent individual treatment. This has been going on for five months. Meditation and treatment have become a vital support for me. It is not a question of just sitting still, each one for himself, but of a group that becomes a praying community and sends out broad circles of intercession, as if a pebble were thrown into a pond. To begin with, one's own forces are activated, collected in order to channel the entire being, body, soul and spirit, to God through Christ. For me, this was the beginning of a period during which my faith matured. This also results in a marked calming and increase in optimism in those around me. The warmhearted way in which the healer shows her interest in each one of us and her laying on of hands work wonders with me. Such words as, "We must allow ourselves to be used by others, even if things are not going well for us, we must pray for the sick—we must be there for the poor—we must transmit joy—we must not brood . . ." and many like them are spoken in the course of meditation.

With her I am learning to track down my negative thoughts—for these are always with us—and to turn them to a positive attitude, also in the context of the healing of our child. At one time during treatment Mrs. Riedel relieved me instantly of the pain of a kidney stone that had not left me for a whole week. When I thanked her she told me that I should thank God, not her.

Mrs. S. in B.

Depression following a Sister's Suicide

During my weekly visits to the sessions of healing meditation and subsequent treatment by Mrs. Riedel for the past two months many positive changes have occurred in my body and soul. Above all, there has been a positive change in my disposition, I have gained positive impulses in the running of my life, confidence, strength and hope, self-assurance, self-respect and love for my neighbour, a sense of religion, a broadening of consciousness, courage and optimism; a sense of being borne along and yet of having solid ground beneath my feet; acceptance of both living and dying; the overcoming of hate, guilt and other negative feelings; the ability to forgive and to let go; the ability to live in the present and constantly to start afresh; understanding for others and their sufferings; and a marked improvement in the depression and other psychosomatic disturbances from which I am suffering. I am

profoundly grateful to Mrs. Riedel for all these experiences, the more so
since not only I have profited from them but also my family and all
those with whom I come in contact.

Mrs. S. in N.

Thank you very much indeed for the wonderful sessions of healing
meditation during the festive season (Christmas and New Year
meditation), for the privilege of being with you and your guests. Thank
you for your affection and your generosity—your efforts on behalf of
others are quite simply overwhelming!

My life and my entire attitude have taken a positive turn. Thank you
again!

Miss M.

A Consequence of Healing Meditation

When I once again glance briefly at my past I am amazed to see that I
have become a totally different person. There was the examination for
my master's diploma in Berne—I failed because I had lost my faith in
myself. Moreover, I was given no support at the place where I worked.
All the people there radiate nervous agitation and are dissatisfied with
themselves and everything around them. My dear wife and the children
went through a difficult time. The head of the firm did not want to
work with me any longer.

A new start, a new life—that was and still is my theory. We can all
only gain from this. Then something strange occurred. My wife got
Mrs. Riedel to treat our son who suffered from asthma. Today he is
completely cured. My wife persuaded me to take part in this healer's
sessions of healing meditation since a great deal of good was to be found
there.

When we arrived in Lenzburg and entered Mrs. Riedel's house the
waiting-room was pervaded by unusual music. Then Mrs. Riedel came
into the room, bringing with her an emanation that I have truly met in
very few people. There she stood, the woman who has since channelled
my life along positive lines and to whom I have become greatly
attached.

She explained the sense of healing meditation very clearly to all of us.
After the introduction with prayer and singing there came for me that

which was new. The oriental music already brought my body and soul so close together that they might have been the best of friends all my life. A slight tingling above my head told me that something was about to happen. I have now participated in several of these sessions and each time I have made fresh discoveries.

Today, 10th December, 1983, I am convinced that all of us would be a great deal happier if we were to cease tearing each other apart mentally and spiritually. The worst and most bitter war is that against oneself and it follows that the greatest victory is that over oneself.

Meditation has shown me how to see myself. Actions and events take place that leave me amazed every time. I see myself observing in the pictures that appear. These pictures become continually clearer and warmer. I feel awareness and strength growing in me like a tender but extremely resistant flower that pushes out its buds in spring. It is strong enough to face up to the coldest of winds.

I am still too young and inexperienced in this domain but I am nevertheless overwhelmed by a conviction which encourages me to do deeds I should never even have dreamed of earlier. All this I owe to one woman of exceptional spiritual greatness and strength. Her name is Mrs. Madeleine Riedel-Michel.

As soon as my own experience and knowledge have sufficiently matured, I see it as my task in life to help others.

Mr. O. in N.

A letter of thanks from the Philippines

I am glad to be given the opportunity of expressing my thanks to you for recovery from my illness. Thank you and the psychic surgeon, Josephine Sison for the healing powers you have been granted by God.

I should have liked to speak to you in Josephine Sison's Chapel in Barangobong but you were so busy and it is not right to talk in the Chapel during healing. God has been kind in allowing me to meet you and Josephine Sison for you have made me well again through God's goodness.

I visited Josephine Sison several times. I first went to her when I had pains in my neck and could not sleep properly. She removed a "witchcraft" in the form of dried banana leaves and I was subsequently greatly relieved and able once again to breathe freely. The second time I went to her I had pains in my chest. She removed a thick, white mass with tentacles and I once again recovered. The third time I went to her I was accompanied by my daughter who had pains in her abdomen. Clots of blood and a whitish mass were removed and my daughter was much relieved. The fourth time I went to her I took my youngest daughter with me who was suffering from earache. A cricket (insect) was removed and thanks to the help of our heavenly Father my child is now well again. The fifth time I went to her you, Mrs. Riedel, were there to help with the healing. You assisted when I was operated on. Josephine removed blood clots and a whitish mass and "beetle-nut husks". I expect you will remember. I have met many faith healers and psychic surgeons and I know of their astounding powers to heal the sick but the greatest of them all is Josephine Sison for she is a true faith surgeon.

I also met the healer, Dany Silab. I was relieved of my terrible stomach pains. I even went to healers who extracted bad teeth with their bare hands. After the tooth had been removed they gave me salt and vinegar to gargle with and my gums stopped bleeding. There is only the slightest pain during the extraction and after gargling everything is in order again.

According to Josephine Sison almost everything that has been removed from my body through psychic intervention was caused by witchraft, a circumstance that doctors cannot explain. The doctors who came to watch Josephine operating with her bare hands were as yet unable to understand that either, nor the fact that she closed wounds simply by stroking them with her hand.

There are many secrets in the world. I am very pleased to hear that you are writing a book about spiritual healing and that you have been so successful for many years in your own country.

I hope I may receive a copy of your book when it has been published for I should cherish it all my life. My eldest son qualified as a doctor in April. In gratitude.

Mrs. R. E. G., the Philippines.

Report of a Scientist in Germany

Our little son had to have his blood exchanged during the first days of his life. If this had not been done, serious complications would have ensued because of a blood group intolerance. As a result of this measure he appeared to develop normally although he suffered from a speech impediment. As a result he was officially classified as "disabled" and subsequently frequented a special kindergarten and a special school for children suffering from speech impediments.

When he was four-years-old we had him treated for several weeks by Mrs. Riedel and in later years, after we left Switzerland, treatment was repeated a number of times. It was wonderful to see how much good this treatment did him. The fact that our child subsequently developed astonishingly well and now, at the age of thirteen, is frequenting grammar school, is ascribed by us very considerably to Mrs. Riedel's treatment. She told us that she felt how the speech centre in the brain at first seemed dead and gradually began to react and become filled with life.

As a scientist I am accustomed to exact and logical thinking. It is no deviation from the habitual scheme of thinking when I accept that cosmic forces in concentrated form can be applied and that there are people who in some special way have access to these forces.

The fact that these forces are researched precisely in such a materialistically oriented country as the USSR and made available to technical progress must be regarded as further evidence that this is no matter of numinous charlatanry. We are extremely grateful for having met Madeleine Riedel.

Dr. G. in D.

Report from a Clergyman in Germany

Any Christian well acquainted with the Bible who goes to Madeleine Riedel for treatment will recall Christ's words to his disciples when He sent them out on their universal mission upon His Ascension, "They will place their hands on sick people and they will get well." (*Mark* 16:18)

The Bible reports on various occasions about people who, in prayer, have healed and the Apostle Paul counts—as a matter of course—the ability to heal among the graces granted man by God (*First Letter to the Corinthians*, 12:9).

In the course of the centuries many had no idea what to do about all this and banned healing through the laying on of hands to the domain of the sectarian and the parapsychological which could have nothing to do with God or the Christian faith. Anyone making the acquaintance of Madeleine Riedel will quickly be taught otherwise. She heals—and lives in conscious daily contact with God. Sectarian tendencies are conspicuous in her by their absence. What will be found, however, is the struggle for true faith and the endeavour to live as a true servant of God and to use the gift of healing to the benefit of mankind, practising it on God's behalf.

That which until recently was regarded as parapsychological is today more and more being confirmed as scientific and medical. Healing magnetism is physically measurable. In the human organism there are minute electro-magnetic particles which fall into disarray in the case of sickness and can be brought back into order by the correct magnetopathic measures, and this by—measurable—magnetic streams which, as in the case of a magnet, run from pole to pole, from one hand to the other. This knowledge is still very new and is being constantly researched but it is the welcome first step towards recalling from the realms of obscurity a method of healing that has already brought thousands new strength and a return to health.

As a long-standing patient of Mrs. Riedel's I have experienced her faith and her healing powers. With her gift of magnetopathic healing she has laid her hands upon me and I became better.

Dieter Grünewald, pastor.

From the Point of View of a Curate

During the twenty-three years that Madeleine Riedel has been working as a healer I have frequently had occasion to speak to her in my capacity as a clergyman and for a short time I was one of her patients. I knew her family and her parents. I married her to Bruno Riedel on the day that also marked the Silver Wedding anniversary of our beloved "Hermano".

I have always known Madeleine Riedel as a religious woman and have constantly been aware that her ability to heal is, in the final analysis, a gift from God. It is not for her personally but as a help for others. In this way she has worked tirelessly to heal others as I have consistently seen. She has given them courage, encouraged them to think positively and, not least, she has prayed for them. It is with pleasure that I quote here one of her prayers that is evidence of her attitude: "As you do every day, Lord, grant me the great strength to get through today. Grant that I may come a small step closer to you. Let me transmit the great strength I receive from you to my patients who wish for nothing more than to return to health. Amen."

Today it is becoming universally realized that healing cannot be expected only from chemical remedies no matter how helpful these can be in certain cases. God has many ways of helping people. There can be no doubt that the way via the healing powers of a Madeleine Riedel is one of the ways for many people. It is also important here that this is done without presumptuousness and in true humility before God, for all the gifts and powers in Man come from Him. He is a great Healer. I am delighted that Madeleine Riedel works in this sense and without rest. May the selfsame God reward her service with His goodness. I wish her continued success and pleasure in her great activity as a healer and a helper of humanity.

E. V., Curate in W.

V. Interviews

Antonio Agpaoa

Antonio Agpaoa was the most famous healer in the Philippines and his name features in the encyclopaedia of parapsychology.

My meeting with him was gay and relaxed. As I wanted to acquaint myself with his method of working I asked him to operate on my shoulder. This did me a great deal of good.

During this mediumistic operation he sang me a beautiful English love-song! Since the girls who usually sing during operations were not there (this is a source of inspiration for him), he did the singing himself. It was a wonderful feeling and I couldn't help being reminded of our Wildegg doctor, Hans Glarner—now unfortunately dead—who, instead of prescribing medicines for his patients, used to sing to them in his excellent tenor voice in order to wrap them in positive vibrations.

Antonio Agpaoa, known affectionately as "Tony", built a large healing centre in Baguio where people from all over the world came to him. He was the first to make himself available to science and he was frequently misjudged. We owe him a tremendous debt of gratitude for it was he who blazed the path for the spiritual healers and surgeons who were to succeed him. I greatly appreciated him as a spiritual healer and as a mediumistic surgeon. He invited me to visit him again but unfortunately he died suddenly a year later at the early age of forty-two, a circumstance not infrequent in the case of healers.

My meeting with Juanito Flores in the Philippines

When one meets the spiritual surgeon, Juanito Flores, one sees a very shy rice planter who will let you take his photograph—in private—only when you have won his confidence. When he is in a state of full trance he becomes a jolly, joking "Medium Operador" who undoubtedly performs the most spectacular operations for miles around. Juanito is famous for the spiritual injections he gives without benefit of hypodermic syringe—and yet, the prick of the needle is clearly felt. Moreover, he frequently sticks a spoon into the pit of a patient's stomach and spoons blood out. He is the only healer who, on principle, refuses to have photographs taken during his operations since he works in trance and the flash could cause him to fall into a faint. Every patient is required to respect this condition.

The first time I went to Juanito Flores, with my faithful companion, Felipe Ventura, his chapel was filled to overflowing with people from abroad and a few Filipinos. A young man from Mexico lay on the front pew, gasping and wheezing in a heart-rending way. Juanito was already giving his spiritual injections in which one feels the prick of the needle and sees blood seeping.

Very few of the many patients in the chapel had the good fortune to witness his mediumistic operations since, from sixty people, he chose only about ten and these were usually the poorest and the weakest. Since he knew that I was also a healer, he allowed me to watch many of his operations and sometimes even to help him. When the turn of the young man from Mexico came, Juanito's assistant held a Bible over his head and many helpers encircled him, praying and radiating positive vibrations until the field of force was sufficiently strong and Juanito was able to operate. He removed a tumour from the young man's head and another from his chest and drained off the purulent fluid. The youngster gradually became calmer and then the dreadful wheezing diminished. His parents and all of us who were present were greatly relieved and thanked God.

While I was on the Philippines I often met a German doctor who, at that time, was very sceptical. His wife, however, believed unswervingly in the phenomena and had her legs treated. When the doctor was able to witness the spiritual injection Juanito gave and saw the blood running down his wife's legs after she had jumped on feeling the "prick", he gave me a little dig and whispered, "Now I believe!" Later on he himself underwent a mediumistic operation on his shoulder and we subsequently had many interesting discusions. Since then we have corresponded cordially.

Interview with Professor Dr. Esperanza Limcaco, the University of Manila

Madeleine (M):—Professor Dr. Esperanza Limcaco, you are a psychologist at the Philippine University in Manila. I should like to ask whether you can envisage the day when doctors and healers will work together all over the world. This has already been done in England and America for many years. On the Philippines, too, I have seen that doctors are a great deal more open-minded than they were three years ago. Even in Switzerland three years ago we had the first international healers' day in which healers from various countries participated. There were also some Filipinos whose mediumistic operations aroused tremendous interest. What do you think about the possibility of co-operation?

Professor Dr. Limcaco (L):—I believe that this is the best way to help sick and suffering people. There are many reasons why a person becomes psychically and physically sick. He has the best doctors, operations and medicines and still he does not recover—he is given up as incurable. This shows that the patient lacks something and that something is amiss. It is precisely here that spiritual healing would be the ideal complement to medicine. I have seen many examples and shall cite here a single case. My brother-in-law fell seriously ill with cancer of the stomach. A malignant tumour was removed by surgical intervention. He had the best doctors, examinations and treatment in the best hospital in the Philippines, the Makati Medical Centre. But the wound across his stomach refused to heal. The doctors called in many specialists but no one was able to help. The wound remained open and he lost so much weight that he looked like a skeleton. He could no longer eat, sleep or stand and his hair had turned completely white.

I went to see the doctor in charge who was also the one treating my brother-in-law and I asked him how things really stood. The doctor in charge replied, "Dr. Limcaco, you can only wait . . ." "Wait—wait for what?" I asked. "There shall be no more waiting!" I told my sister who was in such a state of worry that she couldn't sleep either, adding, "If that is all they suggest, just to wait—what are we waiting for? The best thing is to bring him home from hospital." So we brought him home. I brought him into this room and blessed him since this room has a particularly good and positive vibration. I use it to meditate in, to relax and for spiritual seances. Then several of my sisters gave him spiritual healing and sent him streams of healing magnetism, prayed for him and blessed him. He was also given hypnotherapy. One day we took him to the Province of Pangasinan to the "Medium Operador", Rosita Bascos, who has since died. She was just as good as Josephine Sison.

She performed a mediumistic operation on my brother-in-law. My sister and I were witnesses. Afterwards the wonder occurred. I told you that he was no longer able to walk, eat or sleep. On the way home through the Province of Pangasinan he suddenly saw cooked corn and he wanted to eat! Imagine! We knew that his stomach was completely empty and that he had not eaten for a long time. And now he was demanding cooked corn! We were quite incapable of discussing the matter—we just gaped and said, "Why not?"

We gave him what he had asked for and he ate it! That was the beginning of his recovery. He rediscovered himself. All that is five years ago. The doctors had already given him up but we told hm we wanted to save him. My sister and I would not have given him up for lost for anything in the world and so we prayed. She prayed by changing the formula in the Lord's prayer, "Your will be done", by simply praying in her desperation, "Father, give me back my husband—I need him!" Today he is perfectly healthy, he feels strong and has been able to start working again.

M:—Do you believe in withchcraft?

L:—Yes, it exists and we can no longer ignore it. I cannot exactly explain it since there is still a great deal to be researched in this domain. Later on we shall know more. But it does happen.

M:—Would you be so kind as to give my readers and all the healers and doctors, therapists, nurses and medical students—all who practise a helping profession—a few encouraging words to take with them along their path through life.

L:—I should first like to congratulate you, Madeleine, on your valuable work. I believe this is very impressive for our fellow men. It is wonderful to know about all you do—and it must require a great deal of energy. There are many unbelievers. However, inspired by what you have written, I can see that a change in our thinking is taking place and that, thanks to your explanations, people will be better able to overcome many obstacles. I am happy to know that you are approaching medicine and the sciences for I have been a professor at the University for thirty-eight years and I teach my students scientifically although I have always been interested in the aspect of spiritual healing. I have frequently been assigned the task of clarifying the relationship beween intellectual science and medical science. I feel we should go into this much further in future. When this is done in a lopsided manner it fails to convince. We must pay far more attention to the entire areas of intellectual science, medical science and the natural sciences, get to know them better and obtain experience with all the aspects. Then we can talk about them reliably and with authority and explain things to people.

Good luck with your work, Madeleine.

M:—Thank you for this constructive conversation.

Interview with Dr. Jesus Lava, M. D., Manila

Madeleine (M):—Dr. Jesus Lava, you are a medical fact-finding expert. Since 1974 you have been director of scientific and psychic research into mediumistic surgery on the Philippines. You are also the co-author of a book published in 1982 and called, *Faith Healing and Psychic Surgery in the Philippines*, written in co-operation with the philosopher, Dr. Antonio S. Araneta. In the past you have also been active politically and have acquired extensive experience in the fields of medicine, politics and now, also, in spiritual healing and psychic surgery. In England, South America and—since recently—also in Switzerland healers and doctors work together. In my work with Josephine Sison I have also seen many a doctor who has come for treatment either for himself or for a member of his family, bringing patients or friends with them. It appears to me that, in this country, the attitude towards spiritual healing and psychic surgery has become much more tolerant and broadminded. What is your own impression as a medical doctor?

Dr. Lava (L):—I shall try to give you an historical survey. When we began our research work on faith healing and psychic surgery in 1975 I wrote to the chairman of the medical association and asked for his co-operation in this research. The chairman ignored my letter. In 1978 I met the new chairman of the medical association (the chairman changes each year). I spoke to him about spiritual healing and psychic surgery and once again asked for co-operation. His reaction was, "It's all a great big swindle!"

In December, 1982 we published the English edition of the book you have just mentioned (and I think you have read it). A few weeks later I was invited to the Medical Association of the Philippines to talk about this subject. In May, 1983 I lectured to the National Medical Association of the Philippines. You can thus see the development of this research work. Well, I can understand my medical colleagues originally qualifying spiritual healing and psychic surgery as a swindle. Today they have evidence in the shape of the many cases of healing as well as of our research that these phenomena exist and can no longer be ignored. My colleagues have now changed their attitude. Furthermore, many doctors in the Philippines have adopted a positive attitude since they discovered that it is not the intention of the spiritual healers and psychic surgeons to oust classical medicine. In other words, there is no need to see any reason for conflict between spiritual healing and classical medicine; on the contrary, there is every reason why the two should work hand in hand. If the one method is not sufficiently effective then the other one can be tried until the required effect is achieved. This gives us the assurance that we need the spiritual method as a complement.

M:—It is inevitable—we must accept all these "Medium Operador" on the Philippines. These mediums have received a great gift from Jesus Christ through the Holy Ghost. What is your experience as a doctor?

L:—I should not like to refute the theory that this gift comes from Christ through the Holy Spirit. For me, this is something which is very difficult to prove—in fact, it does not lend itself to proof. Whatever the source of the gift is I have seen and experienced that spiritual healers are capable people whose abilities grow and develop and are renewed and "recharged" in their intensive meditation. In other words, meditation shows them the way to obtain the healing strength and how, through this channel, to heal and to speak. This is pretty well the extent of my medical observations.

M:—Have you been able to subject to laboratory tests these materializations of tissue which the "Medium Operador" takes out of the body?

L:—Certainly. For a long time we have made many attempts by sending them to the chemical laboratory for testing. At one time I sent a diabetic to the healer, Blance. He removed tissue which materialized in the region of the intestines and I sent this to Dr. Stelter who, in turn, sent it to the medical-chemical laboratory at the University Clinic. The result was—sugar! We also sent tissue to the municipal medical laboratory and in all cases of diabetes it was sugar.

M:—In some operations the "Medium Operador" works inside the body and in others there is merely materialization, that is to say, bits of tissue mixed with blood appear on the surface of the body, even if blood runs from the body. Both forms of operation are successful and of good quality. What is you experience as a doctor in this context?

L:—I should say that it is a question of technique. The healing mechanism is more or less the same. Since we do not yet really understand what materialization is and cannot clearly see that the hands penetrate the body wall, it is all very difficult for us to understand.

M:—What do you think about witchcraft?

I ask this question here and also when I interview the healers because it is the one most discussed when psychic surgery is being talked about. We all have a lot to learn about it.

L:—There are many things that appear in the form of witchcraft. By this I mean that it exists. When people wish to do you a damage by the force of their evil thinking, there is a malediction. My experience has been that people who carry the results of an imprecation in them are ultimately put entirely out of action by this damage. That is to say, they are inactivated so that the evil in their bodies—which must have been low in resistance—can take its effect and destroy the energy fields. When the "Medium Operador" removes the thing involved in the witchcraft from the patient's body, he releases this field of energy and the damage is repaired. At this moment the imprecation returns to the person who sent it. Good has triumphed over evil. The fact that the healer can in fact remove things from the body of a sick person is, albeit, very difficult for many people to comprehend.

M:—Of course it is difficult. However, I have been most interested to see how many gravely ill people—particularly people from the Philippines—have been carried into the chapels and how often the result of witchcraft has been removed. And then, one, three or five weeks later they would all come back, looking healthier and fresher each time. One could see that the evil had left their bodies and their consciousness and they had become healthy again.

L:—I understand. I do not say that it is a swindle but that this kind of witchcraft has a very deep significance. Everything I have seen proves that this happens. I am not unaware of the things that happen. On the contrary, I believe that the best thing for a scientist is to have an open mind and to let things come as they will.

M:—I should like to ask you if you could give my readers and other members of the medical professions, as well as healers, a few positive words for the future.

L:—My experience tells me that we should support the spiritual healers—they have had to suffer and tolerate enough difficulty already. We should complement each other. My impression is that psychic surgeons may be consulted by anyone as a complement to classical medicine so that we may achieve a truly better state of health for everyone. And when one considers the present increase in the prices of drugs, pills and the other forms of classical medicine, I can only say that spiritual healing and psychic surgery can be a great help, particularly for poorer people who cannot afford the methods used by modern medicine.

M:—Thank you for these helpful explanations.

Interview with Mr. Benjamin Felix, Vice-Chairman of the Philippine Association for the Scientific and Psychic Research of Psychic Surgery

Madeleine (M):—Benjamin P. Felix, you are the vice-chairman of the Philippine Association for the Scientific and Psychic Research of Psychic Surgery. What is your opinion of world-wide co-operation between doctors and healers?

B. P. Felix (F):—I have talked to many doctors, above all with many Japanese doctors. The final question is always the same—"Can I learn PSI healing and PSI surgery as well?" Why not? The technique is learnable but everything must grow, above all the development of the soul. The idea of helping is good but this must be done with love. You have to develop your intuition and allow yourself to be guided. However, if you want to help the sick only for your own profit and renown, it all becomes immoral. Every healer and doctor has the opportunity of reaching a higher level of consciousness (expansion of the consciousness). But this must take place in the utmost humility; if not you will be led astray and become arrogant. It is her humility that I value so much in the psychic surgeon, Josephine Sison. Among all the many healers she is one who reaps benefit from her humility and has thus progressed to a higher level of consciousness. Dr. Brosach in Laguna is a doctor and she also helps as a spiritual healer and psychic surgeon. If up-and-coming doctors did not go to university with the idea of becoming millionaires but rather with the intention of obtaining the tools and intellectual wherewithal to help their fellow creatures they would discover just how enriching this is. One can develop abilities and understanding such as this and use them as a means of penetrating disease; for a human being is a spark, a part of God. We talk about strong forces—but Jesus said, doctors will have to learn that it is not the body that counts but that which gives the body life. One day there will be no more war, no more rivalry—only true, universal love among humankind. I have given lectures all over the place on this subject. I have caused whole groups of doctors and scientists to change their way of thinking. As I was leaving they wanted to make me their spiritual leader. I said no, I am not a teacher, I propagate no new religion; one must merely look a little deeper since it is all there. When I was a young man I had cars and things. Today I am no longer a slave of worldly goods. Everything comes with waiting, but without stagnation—let it grow, just let it grow. What does Jesus say? This Word is the Truth and the Truth shall make you free. Freedom is all that counts. God is freedom. That is the objective. Of course there is rivalry between healers, doctors, scientists and metaphysicists. But, in the last analysis, what is it that counts for mankind? Neither metaphysics nor science nor yet religion—all this is merely at the service of humanity. Never let us think that we were born for science or for religion. Science was born for us. Religion was created for us, metaphysics and parapsychology were also created for the service of mankind. It is thus that you must think—then, and then only, will you reach a higher level of consciousness.

M:—Do you believe in reincarnation?

F:—Yes, that is a law and not a question of faith. We all evolve. Everything depends on the law of Karma. No one can forgive you anything. Your actions inevitably fall back upon youself. You cannot influence that which has happened in the past but you can quite definitely influence what is to happen tomorrow. One must do right and allow oneself to be helped. There is a tremendous change taking place at present. A new world is in the process of being created and one day we shall no longer suffer.

Do you know Ramba? He changed his body. He wrote sixteen books in Tibet. It is incorrect to believe that Christ was born as we Christians believe. He was not born, he was created. But Jesus was born and gave

Christ his body. Christ shook humanity awake and he scolded people. But people do not want to be roused from their lethargy nor do they want to change their doctrines. We have to learn to understand God and thus, also, our fellow humans. How can you love God when you cannot even love your neighbour? Heaven, which people are always praying for, looks pretty much the same as our earth. We confuse Paradise with merry-making. Life becomes worth living only when one stands above it. No more hunger, no more jealousy, no more rivalry—that is Paradise, A hungry man wants to eat. We have to look beyond things. There is only one life but it has many forms. People are not afraid of death but of losing their friends. People are afraid of disease. So heal yourself! Heal your thinking and everything you do, do for your self!

M:—Thank you, Benjamin P. Felix, for giving me and my readers an insight into your thinking and allowing us to benefit from your rich experience.

Interview with the Psychic Surgeon, Virgilio Gutierrez, Manila

I had to wait three years for this meeting! How I should have liked to make Virgilio's acquaintance earlier—for years I had heard so much good about him and so much confirmation of his successful healing reached my ears. But whenever I wanted to meet him he was abroad.

This time, however, the 1984 Easter week was on my side. Quite unexpectedly, we received a visit from this great "Medium Operador" on 18th April, the day our new mountain chapel, "El Paraiso", was consecrated near the caves in the Province of Quirino. I was completely amazed and delighted to see at his side the Swiss healer, Bernhard Zumsteg from Muenchwilen in the Canton of Aargau, who had been seeking me feverishly in the mountains and caves and had now at last found me, together with the healer, Saitama, from Japan and the Japanese ecclesiastic, Futoshi Aikawa. They, too, were engaged in recharging the batteries of their healing forces in the Philippine caves so that we kept on meeting each other. Two months later Virgilio invited me to Manila and I had the privilege of being present at his house and in his chapel during treatment and mediumistic operations. Virgilio is certainly one of the most sensitive of all the psychic surgeons I have met, apart from the Brazilian healer, Lourival de Freitas. For a long time Virgilio was incapable of performing psychic operations. He was already twenty-eight years old and for the first time had fallen passionately in love with a beautiful girl whose father unfortunately refused to accept him. Thus, this love was violently torn asunder. Virgilio could not and would not understand this, yielding totally to his unspeakable spiritual pain so that he was completely blocked. But his spirit wanted to advance another step towards higher consciousness so he started once more to work, to heal and to operate. At the same time this was the beginning of a successful international healing career. Today he is happily married to another "Medium Operador" and has two small children.

Madeleine (M):—Virgilio D. Gutierrez, since when have you worked as a spiritual healer and psychic surgeon?

Virgilio (V):—For the last twenty-seven years. First of all I was a medium and I went into trance. Later on I devoted myself entirely to psychic surgery. I received transmissions from more highly-developed beings.

M:—Do you have to prepare yourself for an operation?

V:—Yes, indeed. In the morning when I get up I already start to pray and ask God for his protection and guidance. I need to direct my entire concentration and all my energies towards the act of healing ahead.

M:—What is your experience with doctors?

V:—Many doctors and scientists have been observing my work since 1972. For example, there were six patients with kidney and gall stones. After the healing they had to be X-rayed. The stones had disappeared. All the tissue was checked and the results showed that it derived from the patient.

M:—Before Easter do you go to the Philippine caves in order to "recharge the batteries" of your healing powers?

V:—Yes, I always do that. I fast, obtain new healing powers and penetrate more deeply into the secrets of life.

M:—What precisely is psychic surgery?

V:—Well—the first case was Adam for, as he was sleeping, God took out one of his ribs. That was already psychic surgery. During these mediumistic operations one must concentrate very hard indeed and allow oneself to be guided by a deep, unshakeable faith with a strong, devoted love of one's fellow human. Love—and you can heal!

M:—Then, is psychic surgery a great gift from God, granted through the Holy Ghost?

V:—Yes, it is a great gift. The disciples were chosen. Many were called, said Jesus, and few were chosen. Thus, psychic surgery is a gift granted to just a chosen few.

M:—Can you see the patient's aura?

V:—Yes, I can. I have to examine the patient first. I have found that there are many people who are not really ill at all. They just pretend to be ill—sometimes even for fun. If one could not see the aura one could sometimes start doubting—one almost needs to have clairvoyant powers.

M:—For the last three years I have found that the patients are better informed and that the doctors and scientists have changed their attitude in a positive way. Have you also noticed this?

V:—Yes, they are well-informed through books that are read with interest. Also through the many cases of healing that people have heard about from friends and acquaintances. But there are also people who expect too much and are disappointed, even after healing has taken place. We must not forget that there are Karma Laws which we have to respect (the laying-on of hands). And in cases such as these even we spiritual healers and psychic surgeons are subject to limitations.

M:—Do you think it is necessary for the patients to believe in God?

V:—No. After all, I can heal children and animals and they have no belief.

M:—Are your Sunday healings different from those you perform on week-days?

V:—Nothing is different when I am in this climate. But if I leave this country I first have to adapt myself to the different food, climate and people. This takes about two days.

M:—Are you in a trance when you operate?

V:—Yes, earlier on, when I was just beginning, I was in a state of full trance. But today it can happen that my hands tell me what to do.

M:—Do you believe in reincarnation?

V:—Oh, yes. I have believed in reincarnation since my earliest youth, before my father introduced me into psychic surgery. For the faults I make in this life—and I too commit faults—I shall have to pay in my next life.

M:—What do you think about witchcraft? This is an important question for us in Europe and it causes the most discussion. I know many doctors who do not believe that this exists until they have acquired the necessary experience. Then they change their minds. It would be interesting for my readers if you could explain what this is.

V:—There are two forms of witchcraft—black and white magic which correspond to the good and the evil. Black magic can implant something in the body which can easily cause damage. X-ray pictures will make this visible. Things were found that were not there before, this has been scientifically proved—for example, an ordinary stone from the road.

M:—Do you train young healers?

V:—Yes, I train healers inrrespective of their confession in so far as I can find the time and am not abroad. Unfortunately many foreign healers have forgotten that I was once their teacher. For this reason I train only those who honestly desire to join the brotherhood of spiritual healers. We are living in the Age of Aquarius when everything is slowly being transmuted from the physical to the spiritual. A tremendous, general change is taking place. Science can explain why certain islands sink and others appear. The Age of Aquarius also has a great influence on the weather.

M:—Could you say something positive for my readers with regard to the need for co-operation between doctors and healers?

V:—For various reasons I am already working with six doctors—an internal specialist, a cardiologist, a paediatrician, a brain specialist, an ear, nose and throat specialist etc.

I hope that the healers will be willing to co-operate with the doctors in order to contribute to improved understanding and to tend the love of God together. This co-operation would help people understand the truth.

My long experience has taught me that there is not just one life—there is life after death.

My third book is entitled, *Life after Death*, and comprises twenty chapters, among others one on, "Why People Fall Sick", and on healing. There are various kinds of spiritual healers and psychic surgeons. The spiritual healer can see what is wrong with the patient. His hands are guided by the spirit to the root of the disease. Anyone born to be a spiritual healer or a psychic surgeon can become very famous. But this can also be very dangerous if one is led into false paths and engages in healing "business" and management. God said that when one does good one acquires charisma. Healing patients is easy since the root of the matter lies in wrong thinking. Healer and patient must work together, even if the patient is an unbeliever. For God is ubiquitous.

Healing is so successful on the Philippines because we have such good earth radiation, there is a great deal of water around the islands, as well as salt and sun. Then there is our profound belief in God. When we run into difficulties there are always good friends around in whom one can confide one's problems. For you in Europe it is all much more difficult since you frequently do not even know your next-door neighbour and this brings an impoverishment of your Christian neighbourliness.

There was a big healer congress in America to which I was invited. I was very happy to attend and it was all most interesting. People talk about miracles when there is something they do not understand, such as psychic surgery. But the spirit knows no such word since God is everywhere.

M:—Thank you, Virgilio, for the whole of this day I have been permitted to spend with you, in your chapel, during the mediumistic operations and treatment and at your home. I am grateful to you for giving my readers an insight into your work and your thinking.

Interview with the Psychic Surgeon, Placido Palitayan, Baguio

Madeleine (M):—How long have you been working as a spiritual healer and missionary?

Placido (P):—I began as both a missionary and a spiritual healer in 1963, but not yet as a psychic surgeon. I devoted myself more to preaching, the laying-on of hands and other means of spiritual healing.

M:—Did your abilities as a psychic surgeon become apparent only later on? After all, it requires a long period of spiritual development and great sacrifice if one is to be chosen at all.

P:—Yes, it was quite a while later. The gift appeared in a dire situation when I suddenly had to treat the daughter of our jeep driver in the jungle, and was finally forced to operate. I had no choice.

M:—My father once had a similar experience among the Indians in South America. In the emergency he, too, was enabled to operate.

Placido, do you prepare yourself for your mediumistic operations?

P:—At the beginning I always immersed myself deeply in the spiritual world and also needed special blessings. Today, I can switch over at any time when I carry out mediumistic operations, unless I am worried by great problems, a circumstance which disturbs my concentration. Generally speaking, I have strong and strict self-control.

M:—What has been your experience with the doctors?

P:—My first experiment took place eight years ago when the spiritual healers Conzales and Agpaoa were questioned by members of the American Medical Association. Conzales and Agpaoa ran away so that I was the only one available for the interview. I know how to talk about the Bible since I know it very well indeed. My replies fascinated the doctors and they were satisfied.

M:—In 1982 you were also invited to the First International Congress of Paranormal Healing in Basle. What was your impression?

P:—I believe that this meeting with various doctors, scientists and healers from a number of countries inspired all of us to pursue further co-operation. Psychic surgery and spiritual healing are a new and complementary field for both medicine and science. They can no longer ignore us since we are also capable of healing many sick people.

It is high time that they adopt a positive approach to the matter. They doubtless have great knowledge but the time comes when they are glad to have us leap into the breach as a complement to their classical methods in order, together, to achieve better healing results. I believe that what occurred at that time in Switzerland was God's will.

M:—I read afterwards in the newspapers that the mediumistic operations were very successful.

P:—Yes, they were all surprised that the Philippine healers were capable of carrying out mediumistic operations with nothing other than their human qualities. It gave a great many people a lot to think about.

M:—This question is very important for the doctors in order to achieve better understanding. What do you think about witchcraft, manifestations of which are frequently removed from the bodies of patients by the Philippine healers?

P:—Yes, witchcraft is a vicious circle from which it is difficult to escape unless divine strength wins the day. It is difficult to understand but we meet it every day. It is the spirit of evil, destructive forces take possession of a human being.

It exists! Only the forces of good can triumph over it—God's strength. Doctors and scientists can understand this only when they see the source in the spiritual manifestation.

M:—Do you train young healers?

P:—I have trained many healers. However, out of every hundred healers only about seven are successful and particularly gifted. Only those that have a special gift and are chosen can practise spiritual healing and psychic surgery.

M:—What you say is very important since many people in Europe believe that they can make a quick three to four week trip to the Philippines and learn how to perform these mediumistic operations. How wrong they are! Your spiritual healers are already being trained when they are children; to some extent, the gift is hereditary. Above all, you Filipinos have an acuter awareness, the strength to wait and considerably greater faith than we Europeans. You patiently let these healing powers grow through the years, helping, inspiring and mutually "radiating" one another. Very few of these healers are "chosen".

P:—Yes, that is so.

M:—Do you sometimes go to the caves to recharge the batteries of your healing powers, particularly before Easter?

P:—In so far as my spirit prompts me, I can go there at any time. But I only go when I need to and am able to adopt the right spiritual attitude.

We have beautiful crystal caves in Baguio. But I like just as much to go to other quiet places in the countryside where I can cleanse and develop myself spiritually. Quiet, the caves and the wide open spaces are very important to psychic surgeons.

M:—Do you heal only Filipinos or also people from other countries?

P:—I prefer to heal only Filipinos. I love this responsibility towards my own people. I have my own chapel where I bring people in contact with the word of God, strengthen them in faith, hope and love, help them and do all sorts of other good things.

M:—I have seen during the last three years that people are no longer so greedy for sensation and disruptive but that they are better informed, full of confidence and well prepared for the mediumistic operations.

P:—Yes, people's understanding and knowledge have developed. When the patients understand what spiritual healing and psychic surgery involve, they co-operate better. They open their spirits and experience peace within themselves. The most important task of spiritual healing and psychic surgery is not only the correction of the physical well-being of a patient but also his spiritual release.

M:—Do you think it is important to believe in God?

P:—100% yes, since it is already written in the Bible. Those who have no faith do not recover. However, I think a lot of people who say they do not believe nevertheless accept God in their secret hearts.

An example: when I was treating Dr. Harry, an Australian, he told me that he did not believe in it. Why, then, did he recover?

I told him that, deep down, he believed and hoped for healing.

M:—Is the healing you perform on Sundays different from that which you perform during the week?

P:—Yes, on Sundays I concentrate on spiritual healing. I should like people to concentrate more on spiritual healing than on psychic surgery. I feel that spiritual healing through prayers and the laying-on of hands is considerably more successful since people open their spirits more in this case and are correspondingly more receptive. They also take more time for this. That means that they take a big step forwards on their spiritual path.

The mediumistic operations are doubtless also good but here people believe that they have no part in the healing since it is the healer that does all the work. But this is not so! God does the work, I am just His instrument, but the patient must also work if he wants to stay healthy. If people would only learn to understand all that a bit better! For this reason I am more interested in spiritual healing than in psychic surgery.

M:—Are you in a state of full trance or semi-trance when you operate?

P:—I am automatically guided. It is a normal state of trance for so long as I am in this opened spiritual channel everything I do is in keeping with divine guidance.

M:—Do you know precisely what substances you remove from the bodies of your patients?

P:—No, because I haven't studied medicine. My spirit guides me and it knows what must be removed.

M:—Do you believe in reincarnation?

P:—I am still studying it. I have an open mind on the subject but should prefer to express an opinion only when I have completely understood it.

M:—Placido, in conclusion, could you say a few positive words for my readers and for the doctors and healers?

P:—In America people are very receptive for this form of healing. I believe that, one day, spiritual healing and psychic surgery will be completely accepted, even by doctors and scientists, particularly in view of the results achieved. There is no reason not to believe this. The only way for anyone interested to develop himself is first of all to concentrate on the mental energy. This energy is very important since it makes us purposeful and affords us a positive attitude to our Creator. And when I say Creator I mean the all-powerful, all-knowing, all-loving and eternal God that created every living thing and keeps it alive. This deep confidence and the love of God must be developed since these are the sources of healing, of life. If you can consciously accept this a great many other things in your life will quickly be put to rights. Jesus Christ said that we must accept God the Father in all his justice and by that he meant that we should understand all this and practise it in our daily lives.

Thus, I say to the doctors and healers that healing needs confidence, hope, love and a deep interest in the return to health of the patient. For this reason I should like to shake all doctors, therapists and healers out of their lethargy if they fail to tread this true spiritual path. I am sorry to have to say this and it makes me sad. However, I hope that one day they will see their faults and errors and recognize the right way.

Let us thus work together in confidence, love, dignity and devotion to the glory of God and bear these words more carefully in mind in future.

M:—Thank you, Placido, for this frank discussion. I, too, should like to arouse people to awareness of the state of things. Above all to make them more joyous and ready to accept life, to be more loving and courageous, to advance together and to be there for one another.

Psychic Healer and Exorcist, David Oligane, and Spiritual Healer, Ben de Vera, in the Philippines

When I first met David Oligane in 1981 I was aware of feeling very safe in his fatherly presence. We talked for a long time. He invited me to come again in three weeks' time as he often worked in Manila. Thanks to a happy coincidence I met him and his companion, the spiritual healer, Ben de Vera, in an hotel in Urdaneta. A man suffering from cancer who had very little time to live since he was a terminal case full of metastases, had invited me to this hotel. His young wife was with him. He beamed at me saying, "I have had a wonderful day today for two healers treated me simultaneously, prayed with me and sang during the treatment!"

It was the first time that I had seen this very sick man so happy and relaxed. His wife, too, was relieved and they invited me to their room where they awaited the healer. Against all expectations I thus met David Oligane and his companion earlier than we had planned. They invited me to attend the meetings twice a day. I spent precious, happy and interesting hours with these two and their patients. David operated, removed stones and applied cupping-glasses. I was constantly amazed by the cheiroplastic incision which resulted from the strong magnetism of his hands as if made by a well-guided scalpel. Now and again he released a patient from some form of witchcraft. I have seen a patient's body twist and turn with pain and afterwards become greatly relieved. Ben de Vera took care of the post-operative treatment with his healing hands and prepared ginger for a compress on a diseased joint. This was very effective when left in place overnight. During treatment he often sang to the hearts and souls of the sick people, making them aware of God and his unending love. I could see how the faces of some of the grievously sick people lit up and how many eyes were made to shine again.

Interview with David Oligane in Taboy, Pangasinan

Madeleine (M):—David Oligane, you live in Bo. Taboy Asingan, in the province of Pangasinan in the Philippines. You have a reputation as a spiritual healer and an exorcist that goes far beyond the national borders, and are famous for your cheiroplastic incision. The cupping-glasses you often use during mediumistic operations were a source of amazement to me.

How long have you been working as a spiritual healer and "Medium Operador"?

D:—Uninterruptedly from the time I began in 1955 until today. I am very happy to be able to help so many people.

M:—Do you sometimes also heal abroad or do you only work here?

D:—Not only here since I am sometimes invited as on the occasion when you saw and heard me at the 1st International Congress of Paranormal Healing at the NATURA in Basle.

M:—Yes, I remember very will. You, Placido Palitayan and Victor Dewag worked together with doctors, with healers from England and with the Swiss healer, Fred Wallimann. Can you tell me your impression of this congress?

D:—Yes, it was a wonderful feeling. I saw so many people and was permitted to treat a lot of them. I felt that the doctors, the journalists and many other people were very interested in spiritual healing.

M:—I read later in the newspapers that the mediumistic operations were a great success.

D:—I did my share with great pleasure. It was wonderful to be able to demonstrate this kind of healing to the Europeans. I should like to see these people again one day, not because they were healed. It could happen that they become ill again because of negative outside influences, for we are all made of flesh. It would therefore be important for these people to continue the practical treatment.

M:—Do you make any special preparations for your mediumistic operations?

D:—Yes, of course. I cleanse my spirit, my soul and my heart through meditation.

M:—What has been your experience with the doctors?

D:—When I was in Europe many doctors invited me to the University of Erlangen near Nurembourg in Germany. They gave me the opportunity to speak to them and I told them, "Spiritual healing is for us all and sometimes we need you. Let us therefore give of our best for humanity that needs us." I also said to them, "Please do not be prejudiced against our spiritual healing and mediumistic operations, but study them. They are there for all of you, for people that long for them. Humanity will be grateful to you if you could show more understanding in these matters."

M:—Can you tell me something about your work?

D:—At present my work consists not only in operating on and treating people but also in explaining to them about God, the Bible and the immutable laws, about the meaning and aim of our life here on earth and that which will follow.

M:—Yes, I also think that people should open their spirits more than ever. But during the last three years I have seen a very considerable change in the attitude of those seeking help. They are much better informed and have profound confidence while the people who came to us earlier on were more prone to sensationalism and far more critical; they disrupted the atmosphere surrounding the healer. I believe that the books written by Dr. Hans Nägeli-Osjord, Dr. Alfred Stelter, Gert Chesi, Jaime T. Licauco and Rudol Passian have contributed to improving people's understanding.

D:—Many people have no idea what psychic surgery is all about. But they are full of hope and confidence that they will be healed—and they *are* healed. Of course, there are well-informed people who are also healed. But let us be frank and see our life-destroying sicknesses! There are two kinds of sickness, the physical and the spiritual. When the two occur together the patient must be treated physically and spiritually. I should like to draw doctors' attention to this circumstance.

M:—Is it important that the patients believe in God?

D:—But of course, since the spiritual healers obtain their gifts from God.

M:—When you operate, David, are you in a state of trance?

D:—In a state of semi-trance.

M:—Do you know exactly what kind of substances you remove during you mediumistic operations?

D:—Since these psychic interventions are in no way to be compared with classical surgery I am unable to describe exactly what it is I remove. They are mostly bits of tissue, stones, clots of blood, etc.

People who are interested in such matters must have seen and experienced them for themselves to be able to believe in them.

M:—How many bodies do you believe we have?

D:—We have three bodies—the physical body (the material one), the mental (intellectual) or immaterial one and the spiritual one.

M:—Do you believe in reincarnation?

D:—Of course.

M:—I also believe in reincarnation. Many years ago I acted as a medium for Markus Brogle, the reincarnation research worker in Switzerland. The results were both interesting and revealing.

What do you think about witchcraft which you remove in the form of blood-soaked substances from the bodies of grievously sick people during mediumistic operations?

D:—Some people believe this exists and others do not. The doctors, in particular, are sceptical, apart from the scientists who have examined the whole question. But I tell the doctors that this is a disease of the spirit which must be treated. Afterwards the doctors are always very interested. I explain everything to them and demonstrate it all to them. in the end they can see it for themselves and recognize the truth.

M:—Yes, during my daily co-operation with Josephine Sison I was able to see many cases of witchcraft with my own eyes

Do you train young healers?

D:—Of course I should like to do this. In particular I should like to show the children just what a responsible task lies ahead of them when they tread the path of spiritual healing so that they know what must be done when I am no longer here.

M:—The relatively few psychic surgeons here in the Philippines have received a great gift from God, as also have the healers who do not operate. Would you be so kind as to say a few words for my readers and for the doctors so that we might be enabled to advance together in our work for the good of mankind.

D:—Yes, I think that this path will be opened to us for I saw in Europe that many of the doctors are also interested in spiritual healing and psychic surgery. I am very glad to know that healers and doctors will one day officially work together since this will bring great benefit to people. Let us set aside envy and jealousy and become aware that the most important thing in our lives is love. So let us understand one another and work together for the good of our patients and to establish the power of good upon earth.

M:—Thank you, David Oligane.

D:—Let me say a few more words to my friends in Europe, my former patients and to everyone who believes in spiritual healing—and even to those who do not believe. I have already said that there are two sorts of sickness, the physical and the spiritual. Should the day come when you need me I shall be there to help you. Do not be afraid to come to me since it is very possible that I can help you. Doctors and healers are devoting themselves to this and making it their life work. Let us help each other and live in peace with one another. Let us learn from each other. We all need both medical and spiritual healing. The doctors are mankind's greatest helpers and they do a great deal for their patients. However, if they knew more about spiritual healing and were more accurately informed they would be able to understand their patients better and help them even more. I wish and hope that the day will come when God will permit our great doctors and us little healers to stand and work together in order to overcome all the sickness in the world. A most cordial thank you to all my friends and everyone in Europe. I love you all. God bless you.

The Spiritual Life of Josphine Sison, Barangobong

Josefina Escandor Sison, the eldest of seven children born to Conchita Tabigne and Guadancio Escandor, was born on 1st November, 1941, in Cabanatuan City, Nueva Ecija, in the Philippines. She was already aware of the Holy Ghost as a child and has been guided

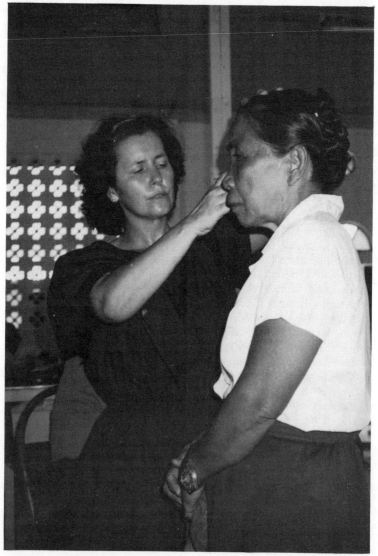

Madeleine giving healing treatment on the Philippines in 1984.

by a direct voice throughout her life. At the age of thirteen she received her first examination and instruction in meditation, fasting and prayer. Irrespective of the fact that her family did not at first understand her, she practised obedience to the inner voice. She says she is happy to obey the will of God in spite of the facts that, for a period of three years, she was forbidden to speak more than seven words a day. This task assigned by God was a difficult but not an impossible one. When Josephine was sixteen years old she was instructed to go among her fellow countrymen and preach the Gospel. During this time she often walked many miles since she preached and taught in the villages. She found little physical comfort on her way and was forced to make many sacrifices. But her life was full of joy because she was at peace with God.

After she had spent many years performing difficult tasks and had commenced spiritual healing Josephine was given the gift at the age of twenty-two of removing disease from the physical body through psychic surgery. It is also possible for her to heal people by looking into their eyes and laying her hands on them or even by her mere presence. Although at first she was able to open the bodies of only three people each day, this ability gradually increased. It soon appeared that there was no limit to the number of patients that flocked to her. At present she is considered to be the healer and psychic surgeon with the fastest-operating hands in the Philippines. On Sundays she will sometimes treat as many as 400 people. Sister Josephine, whom we all affectionately call "Pining", is one of the few healers who works seven days a week and treats all the people from at home and abroad who come to her. These are mostly poor Filipinos but people from all over the world have found their way to Jospehine's house situated on the Pangasinan plain, in a region where psychic surgery first began as a result of the positive earth radiation. Although she never makes any charge for her services, the people give her something since they understand the law of compensation. These donations help her to continue her work. They have also helped her to build a beautiful chapel in Carmen in the Province of Pangasinan and, more recently, also in Aglipay in the Philippine mountains near the caves where the people come every Sunday to pray and be healed.

While "El Progresso" was being built she received special instructions from her guide and protector, the Archangel Michael. A great many people were overjoyed when the chapel was completed on Easter Sunday, 15th April, 1978. In addition to the many healers she has trained Josephine Sison is frequently assisted by her husband, Santiago, whom she married in 1970. They have two sons, Zorobabel, born on 1st December, 1972 and Emmanuel, born on 16th October, 1974. Although the children are still very young, they are both already spiritually active and people say that one of them will at some time carry on his mother's work. When Josephine is questioned on this subject she replies that it is God who does the work and that she is merely His instrument. There is no such thing as an impossible situation for the patients since healing depends on prayer and the attitude of the sick person, as does also the time it takes for him to be healed. Spontaneous healing takes place in only about 2% of all the cases. It is advisable to have several treatments at two-day intervals. However if Josephine Sison tells you that a single treatment or operation be sufficient then you must accept her word and let the intervention take its effect. She also requires that the patient pray before treatment or operation and ask God for forgiveness for all the mistakes that gave rise to the diseased state. "Forgive everyone who has hurt you and send them love. Change your way of life by putting God first and keeping His laws. Listen carefully to those who preach His Word for only thus will you understand God's laws. Be obedient to the Holy Ghost. God bless you all!"

Anyone seeking healing must first receive instruction and be willing to hear the messages given them to help their spirits. Anyone requiring teletherapy should send a recent photograph bearing name and address and a description of the sickness. The sick person should then pray and meditate daily and read one of the Psalms in the Bible. This should be done for thirty days at 9.00 p.m. Josephine also insists that people seeking healing change their habits since it is these that have brought about the health problem. A new path to God's kingdom must be sought and found.

Among Josephine's amazing healing activities is the materialization and dematerialization of sanctified cotton wool saturated with coconut oil which she puts into the body in order to "absorb" the disease. She says that the cotton wool also serves as medication. She has mastered the transport of the cotton wool from one eye to the other and from one ear to the other. In the cases of many people she removes this cotton wool a few days later. In other cases she leaves the cotton wool in the body where it dematerializes of its own accord. This method has been examined by many scientists.

Interview with the Psychic Surgeon, Josephine Sison

Madeleine (M):—In 1982 and 1984 we worked together for more than six months. I helped you to prepare the patients for the mediumistic operations and I prayed with them. We spent many weeks in Diseluad-Aglipay in the province of Quirino in the Philippine mountains where we meditated together in the caves and healed the poor mountain dwellers. Would you please tell my readers about your impressions.

Josephine (J):—I am prepared to have other healers, like yourself, to participate in whatever I do, wherever I go. I am interested in having you at my side during the wonders Jesus Christ performs through my hands. For this reason I am happy to have brought you to the mountains and the caves to take part in this meditation. This was the first place where, as a young girl, I spent so much time meditating, praying, fasting and sacrificing in order to receive strengthened healing powers. I welcome people like you who honestly and devotedly work for the suffering and open their spirits so that this kind of event can become more successful and be further developed. This is a holy place, the place where I have received these powers.

M:—During our daily work together I meet many doctors, scientists, philosophers and medical students who submit to treatment and mediumistic operations at your hands. Sometimes they bring relatives, patients and friends with them and the atmosphere is always gay and pleasant. I am aware of a deep understanding for your work. What is your own experience with doctors?

J:—I am always pleased when these people come to me. I am continually asking Jesus Christ to hasten the day when our doctors and spiritual healers officially work together since they can all save people's lives. This is the reason I know there is no problem. As soon as the doctors permit us to work together officially we spiritual healers shall be very glad.

M:—In your daily work you do not only perform spiritual healing and mediumistic operations, you also bring about the de- and rematerialization of sanctified cotton wool and coconut oil which you cause to disappear in the patient's body and which serves as medication. This method has been tested by many scientists, even by radiology. This is something that interests and fascinates me every time I see you do it. Can you tell me how long you have been using this method?

J:—It is a long time since I received this gift. It happened after I had been performing mediumistic operations for some time. There were some substances that came out of the patient's body. Three or four years later the Holy Ghost sent me back to these caves and permitted me to receive yet one more gift and that was when it happened. I completed my task in the Philippine mountains and then came the time when I was able to carry out this treatment involving the cotton wool. However, I can do this only when the Holy Ghost allows me to and this does not happen very often.

M:—You were very young when you took upon yourself this tremendous task and responsibility. Can you tell me whether you were first of all prepared by the Holy Ghost or whether your ability to perform these mediumistic operations suddenly broke through via the divine channel?

J:—I heard the voice that suddenly told me, "Josephine, Josephine, Josephine, I sent you into this world to fulfil special duties for the wisdom of God on earth."

M:—You are also going to write a book entitled, *God does the Work—I am only His Instrument.* I am very pleased about this since I believe that you have a great deal to tell people to enable them to become more open-minded in their attitude and strengthened in their love of God.

J:—I am sure of this, Madeleine. But before I write this book I shall prepare myself well through fasting and meditating.

M:—Just as I did. What exactly is the witchcraft they talk about here in the Philippines that you sometimes draw from the bodies of very sick persons in the form of various objects? This is a procedure that has so far been very difficult for the doctors to understand, especially those in Europe. I am particularly anxious to help these people by means of your reply so that they may come to understand. I am personally convinced since, during the time I have spent here, I have seen sufficient cases of healing and I also know that this takes place in South America and Africa.

J:—Witchcraft is capable of entering a person's body at any time. It is a kind of force that derives from the Devil. The Devil symbolizes all that is evil—destruction and malediction and all negative forces. For this reason any form of witchcraft is a disease that can attack the whole body. If it is not taken out in time it can lead to malignant cancers. The only thing that can help these people is the power of God because we know that God overcame Satan. Thus, psychic surgery can help to eliminate this diabolical force simply because God is the stronger.

M:—Do you believe in reincarnation?

J:—Yes, I am convinced of it because I have seen everything that happened during my first and second lives. This is my third here on earth.

M:—How do you envisage the future of the world?

J:—I am sure that things will get worse and worse, especially here in our country, the Philippines. I often receive messages from the Holy Ghost. The present crisis was already prophesied in 1970—hunger and inflation to an extent that we are hardly able to pay for even the barest necessities. These difficulties will shorten the path to the end. The future will be worse. In other countries the governments will wage war on each other. But we always try to pray in order to stand firm. The Holy Ghost said to me that we should pray and pray ceaselessly. But I know that, when sin and materialistic thinking gain the upper hand more and more, Jesus Christ will keep his promise and banish us. The next few years will be difficult for all of us. What I am telling you comes from Jesus Christ. We can only pray and live each day in a way that pleases God.

M:—How do you envisage world-wide co-operation between healers and doctors?

J:—I pray constantly for this and I know that doctors and spiritual healers will one day officially work together. So far it was always the question of the profession, the classification that prevented them from doing this. But I know that one day Jesus Christ will mark us all by means of the Holy Ghost and from that day on doctors and healers will automatically work together. Of this I am sure.

M:—Whenever I saw privation, disease and misery in the Philippines I was nevertheless glad deep inside me to have been allowed to work with you and your team and I have learned that the poor and the sick in this country are in urgent need of help, particularly those in the country and the mountains. If God so wishes, I shall come back to you in order to continue this work, to help and to heal wherever I can and whenever it lies in my power to do so. God bless you, your country and all my Philippine friends. I love you all.

J:—Thank you, Madeleine. I hope you will come back one day to live with us again in the mountain and the caves, to pray, to meditate, to prepare and cleanse ourselves so that at all times we are a true instrument of the Holy Ghost and our own healing gifts. Jesus Christ is always with us. God bless you; I love you very much.

VI. Spiritual Healing
as a Complement to Medicine

When the famous spiritual healer, Tom Johanson, visited me in the Philippines at the beginning of 1982 our discussions gave me the feeling that a tremendous development in the relations between spiritual healers and classical medicine would be taking place in Switzerland. Shortly afterwards Swiss television showed a film called *Hands that Heal,* in which Tom Johanson declared that spiritual healers and doctors had already been working together for years in England, even in the hospitals. Healers and doctors spoke during this programme and subsequently 10,000 enquiries were received from the viewers! The interest of the Swiss doctors increased. Shortly after my return to Switzerland in 1982 Tom invited me to the television studios on Mother's Day where he addressed about thirty-eight Swiss doctors (specialists of all kinds) and healed patients, some of whom had been brought along by the doctors themselves. Tom's video film was shown once again and discussed.

This was a careful, tentative meeting—a "taking of the temperature"—which nevertheless proved to be very interesting and went off harmoniously thanks to Tom's informal manner and positive personality. He had a happy knack of capturing his viewers' attention.

Shortly afterwards I went to another meeting, held this time in the private context of a doctor's own home, where healers and doctors met for an exchange of ideas under Tom's leadership. I took the healer, Marcus Brogle, and his wife, who is a nurse, with me, as well as the parapsychologist and author, Rudolf Passian and his friend, Dr. Beat Imhof. There was an increasing interest in learning more about the phenomenon of spiritual healing as a complement to medicine. A little later the first international congress on paranormal healing took place in conjunction with "Natura" in Basle in Switzerland, an exhibition devoted to propagating a healthier way of life. For the first time healers from various countries and doctors were in official co-operation. Among the healers were three psychic surgeons from the Philippines whose mediumistic operations aroused a great deal of interest.

Very many people were present and the general interest was intense. Each healer was given a group of patients that had previously been examined by a doctor and each member of which was then treated by a healer. It was a very welcome thing for the healers to experience harmony and unity between themselves and the doctors for the first time. This was the start of a new era! Many patients were relieved since, for years, they had been forced to go in secret to a healer. Now it was possible for this to take place officially!

Doctor—Patient—Healer

I should like to describe here how classical medicine and surgery, psychosomatic medicine and healers regard people (i.e. their patients):

Classical medicine and surgery consider a person to be a physical being, although—Heaven be praised—this is soon to change through the advent of holistic medicine. The universities teach medical science but the spirit and the soul are forgotten or neglected.

Psychosomatic medicine regards people as beings whose psychic and physical aspects are inseparable. It endeavours to discover the extent to which the spirit causes disease—and can also heal it.

The healer (be he spiritual healer or psychic surgeon) regards a person as a perfect child of God. He receives wisdom via spiritual channels and tries to eliminate the disease caused by erroneous behaviour and wrong thinking by serving as a channel for divine healing which then serves to restore harmony of the body, soul and spirit.

Even when I was a very young healer I enjoyed the confidence of doctors in my work, a circumstance that profoundly touched me. Since I worked with the greatest discretion, a fact which was much appreciated by the doctors, they often asked me to go to their houses to treat members of their immediate family, other relatives or even themselves. I was also asked to go to the hospitals and even to the intensive-care units.

I remember one case particularly well. A young man I knew had a very serious road accident in which his three-year-old niece lost her life. He was immediately taken to the intensive-care unit of the nearest hospital, suffering from brain injuries, disruption of the central nervous system and broken bones. I was called to his bedside where he lay in coma. Since this young man knew and appreciated me as a healer and had always had great confidence in me, his subconsciousness must have recognized my voice and felt the healing forces I was sending him in silent prayer through the divine channel. From then on he started to recover. He soon came out of his coma and a few days later he left the intensive-care unit and went to another department where he had to lie in bed for many weeks. However, his speech centre was still totally disrupted and he was incapable of speaking a single word, a circumstance that caused him great distress.

I visited him again and all his family were there as witnesses. I knew that the girl he loved very dearly was called Barbara and she came with me to his bedside—in my opinion the best medicine is love. When I had completed my treatment I looked him straight in the eye, held his hands and commanded, "Say Barbara—say Barbara! Look—your Barbara is here—say Barbara . . !" I kept repeating this until he was finally able to speak his first word—and that first word was "Barbara"! Then he fell back on his pillow exhausted and wept. All his relations and Barbara and I stood around his bed and we, too, wept and silently thanked our Creator. These are moments one never forgets.

After that I left the treatment to Barbara who contributed enormously to his recovery. This example shows that the doctors and the nursing sisters did everything, really everything in their power to save a human life. For here spiritual healing had been enlisted as a complement to medicine and it had had an appropriate effect. And finally there was the girl and the love of the young man's family who struggled for his life, not only hoping for his recovery but firmly believing that it would take place. This means that we are all capable of helping someone through love, faith and hope and that this should be happening far more frequently. I would even go a step further and say that there must be many mediumistically-gifted doctors and nurses who should waken the gifts slumbering within them and use them officially, particularly before and after operations, in the intensive-care unit and during convalescence. In other words, we should in future all try to achieve holistic medicine which heals body, soul and spirit in faith, hope and love.

The Nature and Purpose of Spiritual Healing

"For wisdom, which is the worker of all things, taught me: for in her is an understanding spirit, holy, one only, manifold, subtil, lively, clear, undefiled, plain, not subject to hurt, loving the thing that is good, which cannot be letted, ready to do good.

Kind to man, steadfast, sure, free from care, having all power, overseeing all things, and going through all understanding, pure, and most subtil, spirits.

For wisdom is more moving than any motion: she passeth and goeth through all things by reason of her pureness.

For she is the breath of the power of God, and a pure influence flowing from the glory of the Almighty: therefore can no defiled thing fall into her.

For she is the brightness of the everlasting light, the unspotted mirror of the power of God, and the image of His goodness.

And being but one, she can do all things: and remaining in herself, she maketh all things new: and in all ages entering into holy souls, she maketh them friends of God, and prophets.

For God loveth none but him that dwelleth with wisdom.

For she is more beautiful than the sun, and above all the order of stars: being compared with the light, she is found before it.

For after this cometh night: but vice shall not prevail against wisdom." *Wisdom of Solomon* 7:22-30.

Before I began writing this book I had had many enlightening and interesting discussions with healers, doctors, surgeons, psychic surgeons, philosophers, scientists, psychologists, medical students, physicists and chemists from various countries over a period of many years. We talked about disease, its cause and effect, healing, achieving and maintaining wholeness, nutrition, faith, God and the world at large. We talked about the negative influences exerted by our environment that weigh more and more heavily upon us, about affluence and poverty and we carefully compared our experience and observations.

We meditated together upon truth and its endless wealth, and upon wholeness—and we felt ourselves in harmony with the world and the universe. A path fraught with responsibility but spiritually very rewarding lay ahead of me when, at the age of twenty-one, I began to devote my life to spiritual healing from a sense of vocation.

For ten years I was allowed to heal independently at the side of my famous father, the healer and hypnotist Hermano (Hermann Michel). Borne along by the Holy Trinity of God the Father, the Son, Jesus Christ and the Holy Spirit I was enabled to show thousands of sick, disheartened, desperate and spiritually misled people a clear way out of their spiritual confusion, their daily cares and their health problems. I was able to acquaint them with the need for conformity with the immutable laws and the consequences and sequences of these laws. I was able to make them understand that my healing powers were a gift from God and that I was no more than an instrument in His Channel of truth and love—He is the quickening power that performs the healing.

What is Spirit?

"The words I say to you are not just my own. Rather, it is the Father, living in me, who is doing His work. Believe me when I say that I am in the Father and the Father is in me; *or at least believe in the evidence of the miracles themselves.* I tell you the truth, anyone who has faith in me will do what I have been doing. He will do even greater things than these, because I am going to the Father."

"But the Counsellor, the Holy Spirit, whom the Father will send in my name, will teach you all things and will remind you of everything I have said to you." *John*, 14:10-12 and 26 (New International Version).

Always remember that the spirit is all-knowing. Wherever the Spirit of God is—and there is nowhere where it is not—evil will be cast out. As a human being you are spiritually perfect and you should know that in you are love, substance, truth and intelligence for God has wrought you in His likeness so that you may reflect the divine spirit. And in so far as you reflect the creative and spiritual principle, the light of truth and the burgeoning of spiritual ideas shall be revealed in you. Always remember that the Christ Spirit lives in you and blesses the burgeoning of your noble, pure and perfect ideas.

Know that the spirit is translated into reality through you by virtue of love-winged thoughts, energies, waves in the form of strength, presence and power, and be assured that God's Spirit is in you and with you always and everywhere.

"But God has revealed it to us by His Spirit. The Spirit searches all things, even the deep things of God. For who among men knows the thoughts of a man except the man's spirit within him? In the same way no one knows the thoughts of God except the Spirit of God. We have not received the spirit of the world but the Spirit who is from God, that we may understand what God has freely given us.

This is what we speak, not in words taught us by human wisdom but in words taught by the Spirit, expressing spiritual truths in spiritual words." 1 *Corinthians*, 2:10-13.

Healing Through the Spirit

God has given us freedom of will but how often are we guilty of abusing it, of violating the natural order of things and thus losing our perfection-geared existence, our health and harmony? We get out of spiritual kilter and either fall ill or have accidents.

If you want to be healed and recover perfect health, you must learn to recognize the truth, you must liberate yourself and learn to forgive, practise humility and a deep faith in yourself and your Creator and face God in devoted gratitude.

Spiritual healing attends carefully to the purity and prudent care of your thoughts and feelings by teaching you how to recognize your shortcomings, set aside unnecessary feelings of guilt and realize that fear, hate, impediments, disabilities, unwelcome memories and meetings do not derive only from this life but that their source must sometimes be sought in earlier incarnations.

Father, into your hands I commend my spirit. Thy will be done.

All those who are healed have activated their inner healing powers, they have made God active within themselves, renewed their spirits and have returned to observance of the natural laws. Today they enjoy an open, free, cheerful, considerate attitude, they work on themselves daily, live in the present and look to the future, to perfection and to spiritual advancement.

Where could our spirit feel safer than in its *oneness* with our Creator? Blending with His omnipresence, omnipotence and omniscience, we experience this source of light and love which flows quietly and strongly through the various paths of healing, refreshing and revitalizing our lives, allowing us to fulfil our daily duties here on earth with purpose and joy and to recognize the beauties of Nature.

What must the Spiritual Healer Respect in Regard to the Doctor?

In the first line the healer must respect the doctor's long and difficult studies and appreciate him as a helper of humanity. It is already written in the Apocrypha (*Ecclesiasticus* 38:1-4):

"Honour a physician with the honour due unto him for the uses which ye may have of him: for the Lord hath created him.

For of the most High cometh healing, and he shall receive honour of the king.

The skill of the physician shall lift up his head: and in the sight of great men he shall be in admiration.

The Lord hath created medicines out of the earth; and he that is wise will not abhor them.

Was not the water made sweet with wood, that the virtue thereof might be known?

And He hath given me skill, that He might be honoured in his marvellous works.

With such doth He heal (men,) and taketh away their pains.

Of such doth the apothecary make a confection; and of His works there is no end: and from Him is peace over all the earth.

My son, in thy sickness be not negligent: but pray unto the Lord, and He will make thee whole.

Leave off from sin, and order thine hands aright, and cleanse thy heart from all wickedness.

Give a sweet savour, and a memorial of fine flour; and make a fat offering, as not being.

Then give place to the physician, for the Lord hath created him: let him not go from thee, for thou hast need of him.

There is a time when in their hands there is good success.

For they shall also pray unto the Lord, that He would prosper that, which they give for ease and remedy to prolong life."

While I was considering these lines from the Apocrypha I was glad that God had not forgotten the doctors and apothecaries because we all belong together!

The healer must also know that the doctor regards his patients more as physical beings, preoccupying himself with the body and its symptoms rather than with cause and effect. This will, however, be changing with the increasing adoption of holistic medicine. The doctor is just as interested as we are in healing those who go to him for help and the healer should therefore also regard the doctor as an instrument of God working in His divine channel. The healer must realize that people are not only spiritual beings but that psychic shocks, inner conflicts and disunity, power struggles, resentment, hate, envy, jealousy, wrong-thinking, guilt complexes, self-destruction, antipathy and a lack of love of long standing can throw the body out of balance and cause it to lose its natural resistance, making it the prey of infection and other diseases. Particularly the acute, life-endangering diseases and injuries should first be attended to by classical medicine.

But when the patient, the family or even the doctor himself so desire, spiritual healing or psychic surgery can be called upon as a complement to medicine. The success is frequently astounding.

What must the Doctor Respect in Regard to the Spiritual Healer?

The doctor must know that spiritual healing and psychic surgery in no way desire to supplant classical medicine but that they can be their ideal complement.

In the *First Letter to the Corinthians* 12:4-11 (New International Version) it is written: "There are different kinds of gifts, but the same Spirit.

There are different kinds of service, but the same Lord.

There are different kinds of working, but the same God works all of them in all men.

Now to each one the manifestation of the Spirit is given for the common good.

To one there is given through the Spirit the message of wisdom, to another the message of knowledge by means of the same Spirit.

To another faith by the same Spirit, to another gifts of healing by that one Spirit.

To another miraculous powers, to another prophecy, to another distinguishing between spirits, to another speaking in different kinds of tongues, and to still another the interpretation of tongues.

All these are the work of one and the same Spirit, and he gives them to each one, just as he determines."

In other words, the doctor must respect the fact that, in the approaching Age of Aquarius, all the gifts described in the *First Letter to the Corinthians* will develop and reveal themselves more than ever among the people since it is the era of spiritual awareness and brotherhood. Doctors can learn a great deal from spiritual healers and psychic surgeons about the energy fields and their mechanisms, about the spiritual laws that govern things and influence people's health, leading to a positive attitude of mind and feeling, to acceptance of life and thus to a far more rapid recovery of perfect health. The doctor must know that the spiritual healer or psychic surgeon is a person with special sensitivities whose field of energy can be disrupted in the presence of scepticism, harsh criticism and negative vibrations. In other words, the presence of a materialistically-oriented observer with very negative, sceptical and critical emanations can so disrupt the healer's flow of energy and field of power that, under certain circumstances, he is unable to fulfil his task in peace and quiet. While treating a patient the healer does not think only of the diseased, material body, he also thinks of man in the image of God, that is to say of the perfect human being that is and will always remain healthy. For this reason the healer first goes to work on the thoughts and feelings of a patient, sending him health-restoring thought waves. He then appeals to the cells, for cells have a cell intelligence and groups of cells also have an intelligence of their own, an intrinsic, ordered system that Aristoteles called "entelechy". The nerves, too, have their own intelligence as do the glands and the organs. Therefore, if it is possible to mobilize this "body intelligence", as Nietzsche called it, the body can become completely well again when this spiritual order is restored.

What must we both, Doctor and Spiritual Healer, respect in regard to the Patient?

We must respect the fact that it is *his* life and that he is free to make of it what he will. The person seeking help should be able to decide freely which therapy he requires and that to which he feels most drawn. It should be possible to speak about all this in respect and dignity to his doctor, therapist or healer.

There should be neither envy nor jealousy between doctors and healers since the only important, indeed the decisive thing is that the person seeking help be aided. It is entirely immaterial whether classical medicine or surgery, spiritual healing or psychic surgery played a greater part in the healing of a patient since we well know that healing can in any case only commence when the spirit of the sufferer is granted the necessary insight.

It is, however, our duty to explain to the person seeking help the true connotations of health and sickness.

What must the Patient Respect?

As a seeker of help you must know that a return to health requires your co-operation and your determination. You should know that sickness is no more than the personification of wrong thinking. You would therefore do well to transmute your negative thoughts into positive ones by means of daily, spiritual training. It is well worth the trouble! (See the chapter on The Healing Process as a Learning Process.)

You must also know that the problems life brings are the true causes of disease which one can damp down but never eliminate by means of drugs and medicines. You must therefore come to grips with the causes of your sickness, clear the decks and find a new way to acceptance of life. All the problems with which life confronts us can be solved by the right attitude and the sickness caused by them thus cured. The power of spiritual and self-healing is present in every one of us. Read spiritual literature for your enlightenment and further training and get to know the natural laws. Always be grateful for everything that happens to you, even for the pain since it is this which shows you that all is not in order and in harmony with the cosmos. In other words, let cosmic life flow into you, for then your spirit will experience the world of truth and divine energy will course through your body. Carry God within you!

When the doctor prescribes medicine for you it is entirely up to your own consciousness whether the substance has a healing or a toxic effect. If your spirit refuses the medicine it can only have a negative effect. But if you adopt a positive attitude to it, it will have a good effect. You should, however, beware of an overdose of medication whose secondary effects could exert an adverse influence on your body (the nerves, the heart, liver, kidneys and blood vessels). The success of the medicine depends upon how the doctor has prescribed it—if you were to lament a little less and have faith in your body's own healing powers, he will prescribe moderate doses of medicine which your body will easily be able to cope with. But if you are always complaining, thus bringing the doctor to the verge of desperation, you will be "overfed" with medicines which in the long run will hurt more than they help. The stronger your determination to recover and your optimism are, the less medication you will require.

Letter of Gratitude to the Psychic Surgeon, Josephine Sison

Today is Saturday, 30th June, 1984, my last day with you in the Philippines. This evening I shall be flying home to Switzerland with the complete manuscript of my book under my arm. This morning I had the privilege of working with you, my dear Josephine, for just one more time. I helped you in the chapel in Barangobong and initiated all the people into spiritual healing and mediumistic operations in English and the local dialect. I prayed one last time with them. There were many poor Filipinos, a few doctors, lady doctors and philosophers among them. They listened prayerfully in complete silence. Once again I saw the tremendous confidence that people feel in your work and in God and I was awestruck, as I have so often been.

Dear Josephine, for more than six months you have made it possible for me to obtain great insight into and great experience of faith healing and psychic surgery. In your presence, in the vibrations of your being, whether in profound meditation in the caves in the Province of Quirino or in the Province of Pangasinan, I have been privileged to write this book which I shall send out into the whole world as a legacy for our patients.

I thank our Creator for the strength, the courage, the wisdom and the intuition that I was permitted to receive daily. I thank Him for the calibre of the people whom I have met during this stay in the Philippines—the poor Filipinos and the people from abroad that now and again find their way to us.

I was happy—with you, Josephine—to have the privilege of leading these people back to the original perfection of their beings through the Word of God.

If it be the will of God, we shall meet again in this "Land of Smiles", this "Pearl of the Orient". May God bless and keep you and all those you hold dear.

In deep gratitude, devoted friendship and Christian love,

Your Madeleine.